# PORTRAIT OF THE SPEY

# *Portrait of*
# THE SPEY

FRANCIS THOMPSON

ROBERT HALE · LONDON

© *Francis Thompson 1979*
*first published in Great Britain 1979*

ISBN 0 7091 7468 3

*Robert Hale Limited*
*Clerkenwell House*
*Clerkenwell Green*
*London EC1R 0HT*

PHOTOSET AND BOUND BY WEATHERBY WOOLNOUGH.
PRINTED IN GREAT BRITAIN
BY LOWE & BRYDONE LTD.,
THETFORD, NORFOLK.

# CONTENTS

# ILLUSTRATIONS

*Between pages 32 and 33*

*Between pages 96 and 97*

*Between pages 128 and 129*

PICTURE CREDITS

# FOREWORD

It is not given to many rivers to have a rather special relationship with human communities over a period of many centuries and generations. In the time of recorded human history, the River Spey has been both master and servant, dictator and benefactor, tyrant and supplicant. In these roles it has moulded not only the topographical features of the glens and straths through which it runs its length to the sea, but influenced the manner in which communities of humans, fauna and flora have reconciled themselves to its presence. Its importance in the Highland scene has been historic, social and economic; yet, unlike the Clyde, the Thames and other rivers in the British Isles, whose presence in their respective areas are often taken for granted, the Spey often tends to be remote from human awareness and, perhaps indicating its individuality, is still largely untamed. As the following pages indicate, the river has a fascinating history, which is not merely local but has on occasions impinged on national events and often, directly and indirectly, stretched its influence to Europe and abroad. Nature having provided its magnificent wilderness setting, among the best in Europe, has also dictated the river's role. It is this role which is portrayed in the following pages.

## ACKNOWLEDGEMENTS

The writing of this book was both an education and a pleasure. The first because it threw an area of the Highland region into sharp focus and presented the writer with a great amount of fascinating detail, as the Bibliography indicates. Having lived with the material on the Spey valley for some two years, the writer acknowledges the enhanced appreciation he now has of the people who live along the banks of the Spey, without whose help this book would not have been completed. I must first thank the staff of the Elgin Library, who made their local collection available to me, and the staff at the Stornoway Library who went to the trouble of obtaining material for research. Among individuals who offered help in one way or another, with sources and illustrations, I wish to thank Mr Alexander Fenton, of the Country Life Section of the National Museum of Antiquities of Scotland; Mr Alfred Ingram of the Research Exploration Group, Dundee; Mr J. H. Macpherson, Newtonmore, whose knowledge of the area continues to fascinate me; Lieutenant-Colonel Iain Cameron Taylor, Inverness, for his detailed and intimate knowledge of the Highland malt whiskies; members of the Royal Society for the Protection of Birds; and Dr George Waterston and Hamish Campbell, Edinburgh for illustrative material.

# I

## THE SCULPTING OF A LANDSCAPE

To savour the true spirit of any landscape it is necessary to gain the heights of the highest peaks and survey, with an eagle-like eye, the 'prospect' (to use a word which now seems to have gone out of fashion). Indeed, the prospect from a high peak is daunting, scaling the human mind down to a minute speck in a scene where Nature is predominant. Little wonder, then, that mountaineers and climbers aim for the goal that, for a little time at least, liberates them from the ties which organized human societies impose on them; and little wonder, too, that the Grampian Mountains are such a magnet for those who literally take Mother Nature into their arms as they scale yet higher to reach those solitary high places and final vistas. On both sides of the River Spey, mountains rise up from the valley floor to heights of up to 4000 feet above sea level, on the Cairngorms side, like a protective wall, while benches of rock in the valley of the Spey occur up to 1800 feet. The broad high plateaux of both the Cairngorms and the Monadhliaths offer the promise of another world where even life itself is a rarity and those who gain access to them are mere temporary visitors, whether birds, animals or man.

What one sees when viewing the Cairngorm and the Monadhliath mountain ranges is the product of a process which occurred from 750 to 500 million years ago: the Caledonian 'Orogeny', or mountain-building period. During this process, when the earth was nothing but a liquid mass in space, the rock-forming fluid was belched up from the molten material deep in the earth's crust and then gradually cooled.

11

But the process was not so simple as a pot boiling over to leave crusts of solid material. The process also involved the mixing of ingredients which were later to become minerals, and the folding-in of materials over a basic stratum of rock, much like the folding-in of flour into pastry. The Grampian range, of which the Cairngorms and the Monadhliaths form a part, consist of a succession of sedimentary sandstone, shales and limestone, deposited on a basic rock known as Lewisian gneiss, which is reckoned to be as old as 2600 million years in places, the oldest rock in the world. Through time much of this sediment was removed by erosion from weathering and the slow but sure working of rain, rivers, snow and ice. The 'roots' of these mountain masses lie as granitic rock known as 'plutons'. Geology is not without its romantic side, despite its highly technical nature. The name is derived from Pluto, the god of the inferior regions, and is applied to igneous rocks found at some depth beneath the surface of the land or sea, as distinct from volcanic, or those thrown up by volcanic action and consolidated on the surface as they cooled. The Plutonic rocks are more crystalline in nature, a characteristic apparently induced by the greater pressure under which they were cooled and consolidated. The Cairngorm region has several of these exposed tooth-roots and parts of others which are connected to the underlying rock base.

The two main varieties of material which form the plutonic masses are granite and diorite. The former consists mainly of minerals such as potash-feldspar and quartz with some mica. The quartz, a beautiful rock, has a high content of silica, and it is this which lodges granite in the family of acid-bearing igneous rocks, an important factor in whisky-making. As a mineral, quartz is properly colourless; but it appears coloured in various shades of white, yellow, red and blue. Those who have admired the in-depth beauty of the violet-blue amethyst, the rose-quartz and the cairngorm (brown or cinnamon-yellow) will appreciate that Nature has done her work well. Diorite, a variety of greenstone, composed of hornblende and feldspar, has little free quartz, but is in contrast, commonly speckled with many black shiny mineral grains. In some parts of the Cairngorms crystals of feldspar can be found embedded in a ground-mass of smaller-grained crystals. Fresh diorite has a pinkish colouring without many dark minerals, whereas diorite tends to be dull-looking.

Much of the mass of Cairngorm is granite and is in fact one of the largest plutonic masses in the Highlands. Its formation is still a bit of a puzzle to geologists. In the normal manner of the formation of these plutons, only one or two granite peaks should be seen; yet the whole massif is a homogeneous granite lump with little intrusion of diorite; where the latter occurs it is an intrusion.

The high peaks of the Cairngorms are over 4000 feet, and include Ben Macdhui (4296 feet), Cairngorm (4084 feet), Cairntoul (4241 feet) and Braeriach (4248 feet), all of which overlook a lower plateau surface rising to about 2000 feet. Incisions into the plateaux appear as glacially over-deepened valleys, such as those at Glen Muick and Loch Avon, with some sheer-walled corries which often contain mountain tarns.

To the west of the Cairngorms, the Monadhliath mountain range is slightly lower in height, but has similarly stepped surfaces extending from Spey to Loch Ness and is littered with peat bogs and glacial debris, bearing witness to the meeting point of ice from the Ness and Spey valleys. These mountains are also almost wholly based on granite. The peaks lie along the watershed between the Rivers Findhorn and Spey and consist, for the most part, of broad level surfaces with a dominant level of about 1000 feet. There are large dumps of glacial material, with some remarkable overflow channels which cut deep into the basic rock; one example of which can be seen in the Slochd, to the north-west of Carrbridge.

The landscape of the Grampians as we see them today is the product of rain, sun and ice, Nature's agents used to ease the harshness of the original mountain-building process. Some 50 million years ago, a time far beyond the comprehension of short-lived man, the land area of what is now the Highlands was subjected to the smoothing process of massive ice-sheets which covered all of Scotland. These sheets moved outwards from the highest ground to what is now the Scottish seaboard. Evidence of ice action is most easily recognized in the Highlands; it smoothed the original roughness of the rocky peaks and accentuated the existing relief. Over great parts of the granite expanse of the Cairngorms, for instance, the ice left areas of bedrock exposed to the subsequent weathering which can be seen today on the high peaks. Hard rocks, however, tended to retain their original contours while their softer neighbours eroded more rapidly. Glaciers blanketed much low-lying ground with a layer of sand, rubble and rock debris produced by their movement over harder rocks; their slow movement, too, also gouged out many of Scotland's present-day lochs.

One particular feature of the area at the mouth of the River Spey is the low undulating nature of the land and its fertility. This is due to another rock base: the Old Red Sandstone, which occurs on the eastern seaboard of the Highlands from Caithness down to the Moray Firth. This rock is a sedimentary product. Whereas igneous rocks are produced by internal processes within the earth, sedimentary rocks are formed by processes which are active on the earth's surface. The surface of the land is being continually attacked by weathering and erosion caused by rain, wind and moving ice. These agents, when they are helped by chemicals decay from percolating waters, break up even the toughest rock and produce rock waste. This is then carried, mainly by rivers, to be deposited as a sediment at river mouths, in lochs and in the sea. The gradual accumulation, which can be many miles thick, is an excellent base for fertile soil. The sedimentary rocks also contain an important feature: fossils, the remains of animals or plants, usually the hardest parts of the organisms, which tell us so much about life in the earth's formative eras.

The area concerned here is fairly low-lying. Most of the higher hills are around 2400 feet. These include the ridge of the Cromdale Hills which separate the River Spey from the River Findhorn. The prominent granite peak of Ben Rinnes, to the west of Glen Rinnes, at 2775 feet, stands as a reminder, with its attendant sgurrs, of its association with the rock of the Grampians. Northwards from Ben Rinnes, the land falls away quickly in hills below 1640 feet, to the Moray Firth coastline. A great depth of river – and ice-carried material covers lower Moray from the western boundaries of the present district. An indication of the thickness of these deposits, which were dumped against the edge of the huge ice-sheet which is sometimes known as the Spey Glacier, can be seen at Binn Hill near Garmouth, which is composed of some 230 feet of these materials. These deposits have in their time been extensively re-shaped by marine action at the higher sea-levels of late-glacial and post-glacial eras, as well as that of the present day, producing the complex terrace features which merge with those of the lower reaches of the River Spey, and the River Findhorn some miles to the west.

The great age of Strathspey is indicated by the width of the river valleys in relation to the rivers they contain. The solid geology of the district has controlled the drainage. The largest drainage system comprises the Rivers Spey, Avon, Livet, Dullan Water, and the Fiddich. The Spey is, of course, the largest river of the system, rising some 98 miles from its mouth, away in the south-west. For its valley to have attained the proportions of the present day is an indication that the river must have, during its history, cut away all soft rocks between the Monadhliaths to reach the true bed of hard rock. However, the River Avon is interesting because it has actually beheaded the River Don which flows to the east coast of Aberdeenshire; it is reckoned that the Avon cut back along a strike or outcrop of rock to capture the head waters of the Don, the older of the two rivers, which drained eastwards at Inchrory. Thus, the Avon has two sources: Loch Avon and Loch Builg, both deep valley lochs. The Spey, too, has its history of diversion. Northwards at Craigellachie, the Spey is diverted by a fault which runs from Dufftown to the Glen of Rothes. The weakened rocks at this fault zone also offered an easier alternative for the River Fiddich and the Dullan Water, which at one time flowed into the Isla but are now tributaries of the River Spey. When the Spey arrives at its middle reaches it finds itself in wide-bottomed valleys with little gradient and by the time it passes into Moray District it is actively cutting down into the basic rock and taking pot luck with its direction. This latter characteristic is seen in the way the river cuts new runs in its attempt to reach the sea, for, on this low-lying ground, it tends to meander as it flows over the unconsolidated deposit material which forms the coastal plain.

Inevitably the Grampians, including Strathspey, offer many instances of minerals and their economic exploitation. The Cairngorms have long been known for their store of semi-precious stones, mostly associated with granite. Normally, the constituent minerals of these stones are tightly packed together so that crystals are unable to develop a good form or shape. However, cavities in the basic rock, formed as gas bubbles or contraction fissures in the rock, were filled with watery residual fluids in which the crystals grew. Specimens of quartz, rock crystal of up to 50 lb weight have been found, with crystals up to 24 inches long. Where the rock crystal has been tinted with impurities, it occurs in shades varying from smoky yellow to dark brown, the famous Cairngorm stones used in jewellery. Beryl and pale blue topaz are also found. Less exciting, perhaps, is the iron ore which was mined in the Conglass area from 1728 to 1737, to the east of Tomintoul. This ore was mostly hematite, an important ore of iron. The ore was carried by packhorse to Strath Nethy where it was smelted using charcoal from the local forests. The mine was then abandoned but re-opened in 1840 for a short time. Galena, a lead ore, occurs in the Rothes area; attempts were made to extract this material last century but abandoned because extraction proved too difficult. A quartz vein, some twelve feet across, with galena and iron pyrites (Fools' Gold) has been noted by a mineral survey in the Dulnain valley.

Changes in the landscape still occur. One of the major agencies in this respect is the flooding of the Spey valley. For the extent of this area, Strathspey has a most efficient drainage system, associated with a huge catchment area. The result is a history of repeated floodings, and often changes in the flow directions of rivers, and the Spey in particular. It was this fact which has caused the loss of previously reclaimed carse land, notably along the Spey between Kincraig and Ruthven. An unpublished report (Speyside Drainage Report) found that a second reclamation of this land would be quite uneconomic. This area is saturated with chemically rich water and, as on the floor of a main valley, has produced an extensive peat-forming sedge marsh, of the kind known as 'fen' rather than bog. Along the alluvial flood-plain of the Spey valley below Kingussie is one of the largest fens now remaining in the British Isles and rivals those of the Norfolk Broads. This huge swampland ends at Loch Insh and stretches for three miles long by up to one mile wide on either side of the Spey. In the past there have been attempts at drainage and some of the drier areas have in fact been reclaimed to produce pasture land; but the old drains are mostly choked by vegetation and the area often floods in winter. The construction of artificial banks on the Spey and the railway embankment along the northern side have probably contributed to impeded drainage within the Insh fens. This is an ancient swampland; recent studies have found peat eighteen feet deep in one place. At Kincraig the Spey broadens out to form the large and fairly deep Loch Insh.

Other changes in the landscape occur as the result of natural events, such as the formation of gulleys. This is the most spectacular sign of erosion, both geological and accelerated. These often follow exceptionally heavy rainfalls, when the excessive water produces mud-flows on the grassy slopes of the schist hills, to lay bare the subsoil, with its uncompacted sands, gravels and glacial debris, originally covered over with thin layers of peaty soil and thin vegetation growth. An example of the way river banks erode is seen on both sides of the River Nethy, where the water has undercut the face of the river terrace, resulting in debris slides. On the roadside west of the A9 between Newtonmore and Kingussie, there is an example of man's contribution to the changing face of the landscape; while this is small in extent it does demonstrate what is taking place on a much larger scale in other places in the Highlands. Here, a small area of felled woodland has been heavily grazed by sheep. Sheet erosion, where the peaty soil comes away from the underlying rock-soil sub-surface, and the formation of 'bunkers' in the steep slopes, is well advanced. The roots of the former trees are now exposed, indicating some measure of the soil already lost. On the higher slopes of the Cairngorms, the dwarf shrub and moss mat are both taking a heavy punishment from tracked vehicles and tractors, human feet and the clipping action of skis over shallow snow. Road-building has created large areas of denuded and unsightly peat and stony debris which, with one really heavy cloudburst, could start a landslide.

Not three months after these words were written a mountain burn burst its banks and left more than one hundred people stranded on Cairngorm overnight. This was the result of a storm which brewed up early in August 1978, which caused the Ault Mhor burn to be swelled by torrential rain and start a watery avalanche of boulders and rock debris downstream until they became lodged under the single-arch Coronation Bridge. Unable to pass under the blocked bridge the water flooded onto the roadside to a depth of three feet. This road leads up to the Cairngorm ski-lift and was busy with tourist traffic. Although many tourists had left the mountainside in response to police 'flash flood' warnings, many cars were left stranded with their occupants, the latter being rescued within twenty-four hours of their ordeal. In this instance, as was the case some fifteen years ago when this burn changed its direction due to flooding, there were no casualties. But the incident underlined the fact that the possibility of sudden flooding taking away parts of the road is ever present and could in the future take cars and their occupants down the hillside.

The appearance of man in the Spey valley was a result of the potential the area offered for exploitation, as seen in the possibilities for agriculture, themselves related to the soils found in the valley and on the hill slopes. Much of the soils of the higher areas are still in the process of formation. Some are less than 10,000 years old, the result of the rocks being broken down by weatherng and chemical activity and mixing in with the clays, sands and gravels, and are being further aided in their levels of activity by the decay of vegetation. The soils tend to be mineral in content on the higher slopes, but become more organic in content where humus has been allowed to build up successive layers. Nearer the Moray coast, the softer rocks of the Old Red Sandstone have accelerated the soil-making processes and produced the high degrees of fertility as evidenced at the present time in the type of the vegetation cover and crops now being grown. One major feature of the vegetation cover in the area is the old Caledonian Forest, which once covered most of the Highlands and remnants of which are still seen in places in the valley of the Spey. The prehistoric colonization of Scotland began the long tale of forest cutting which has continued until modern times. Then the gradual extension of cultivation caused more forest areas to be cleared, a process not reversed until the eighteenth century, which time saw a new phase of planting and which heralded the beginning of reafforestation and conservation.

Indigenous tree cover in the area can be seen everywhere. The pine (*Pinus sylvestris*) and birch have a long-standing association with the ancient forest cover; the latter are to be found on all poorer thin soils where pine and oak grew formerly, and can be seen growing at altitudes up to the 2000 feet level in the Grampians. Remnants of oakwood forest on well-drained sands and gravel soils are to be found in glens and valleys. The pine in our present-day climate is not able to regenerate itself once cut or burnt. This fact was recognized by the middle of the fifteenth century when legislation was introduced by the Scots Parliament to slow down or halt the destruction of the country's forests. Populated lowlands and straths were being denuded of trees and the process of de-forestation was spreading into the remoter upland areas.

However, there are many stands of pine which are the descendants of the trees of the old Caledonian Forest, some trees being as much as 200 years old. The Scots pine is very much a tree of the granite and is able to flourish on poor soils resting on a layer of glacial drift. On Speyside, pine wood stretches in a discontinuous belt from Glenfeshie in the south west to Nethybridge in the north and includes the famous forests of Invereshie, Inshriach, Rothiemurchus, Glenmore and Abernethy.

The settlements of man have naturally occurred on the valley floor where the soil is richest and at natural nodes, for example where the mountain valleys descend down onto the plains and at the convergence of river systems. Settlements also grew up round a fort or castle, built in areas of comparative agricultural wealth, where the land could be farmed easily and livestock raised with little difficulty. Later settlements were established because of economic activity or, as in the case of Grantown-on-Spey, founded in 1765, the need to create a town to act as a focal point for a small important area which had potential for socio-economic growth. Other settlements grew up with the advent of the railway, with their economies based on tourism. Yet other towns and villages were established to accommodate people who had been cleared from their former lands and because of their potential to act as a work force for the estates. Some towns were set up around a former religious centre; others around a religion of a different kind: whisky distilleries. Thus, the settlements in Strathspey, generally following the course of the River Spey, present a wide range of origins, with the underlying common theme of providing a satisfying environment for life and living as offered by the forces of nature in times past.

The River Spey has always been one of Nature's unruly children, often giving pleasure but equally able to change its character to cause havoc to the settlements along its banks. Particularly in the lower reaches of the river, in Badenoch, the river was ever noted for its frequent flooding. The name Badenoch (Baideanach: the submerged or drowned lands) reflects this quirk of the river, especially on the haughs or low grounds which lie between Kingussie and Loch Insh. There are many records of the Spey floods, some recalling memorable incidents. Draining, as it does, an area of some 1300 square miles of mountainous territory, and a flow of 98 miles, with contributions of mountain waters from numerous tributaries, the volume of water making its way to Speymouth is always considerable. Thus, in times of excessive rains or massive falls of snow in the process of thawing, the river system becomes incapable of carrying the water in their normal channels, and flooding results. Such a combination of factors went to cause the great flooding of the Spey valley in 1829. The first few days of August of that year saw a deluge of water pouring from the skies. In the neighbourhood of Belleville and Invereshie the river widened into a tempestuous sheet of water five miles long by one mile across. In Glenfeshie the inhabitants had to flee for their lives before a wall of water. One sea captain from Coulnakyle, in the Abernethy district, who had in his years weathered many a rough gale, saw his 200 acres flooded so that when the floods subsided only fifty were worth cultivating. "I am satisfied that I could have sailed a fifty-gun ship from Boat of Bellifurth to Boat of Garten, a distance of seven or eight miles." The River Dulnain destroyed the Bridge of Curr, a single arch of 65 feet span in its intent to reach lower levels. In the Abernethy district alone, the floods destroyed 13 bridges, three sawmills, three mealmills and a great many houses, together with the loss of many acres of growing crops. At Inchroy, the River Avon rose to a height of 23 feet. Great landslips occurred; whole farms were swept out of existence and the waters actually created new channels for themselves. The plain of Rothes was completely covered and carried "a heterogeneous collection of spinning wheels, chairs, cradles, tables, beds, chests of drawers and every manner of cottage furniture and farming utensils, all indication in a pathetic way the ravages of the swollen rivers". The streets in the village of Rothes became rivers in themselves, pouring water into the houses. The Bridge of Spey at Fochabers was

destroyed with the weight of water pressing against its support-
ing pillars. It had four arches, two of 95 feet and two of 75 feet
span each. The water rose to a level of 17 feet above normal
and cracked the structure throwing some people into the flood
water when the bridge finally collapsed.

Loch Insh, normally three miles long by one mile across, had
its water level raised to about eight feet.

> The River Feshie ... swept vast stones and heavy trees along
> with it, roaring tremendously .... The crops in Glenfeshie were
> annihilated. The romantic old bridge at Invereshie is of two
> arches the larger being 22 feet above the river in its ordinary state,
> yet the flood was three feet above the keystone. Several sheep were
> found alive on the tops of the trees at the foot of the garden of the
> inn at Aviemore. At the mouth of the river more scenes of
> devastation were witnessed by onlookers. In Garmouth and its
> vicinity about fifteen houses were destroyed opposite to the
> sawmill of Garmouth, where the width of the inundation was
> fully a mile, the flood rose 10 feet 2 inches above the ordinary
> level, and at Kingston Port, where the width is about half a mile,
> it rose 13 feet 9 inches.

So great was the body of water rushing into the sea at
Garmouth that no tide could enter the mouth of the Spey. As
far as the eye could see, the plain was covered with water, and
the beach, in the harbour, and along the sweep of the bay, was
studded with stranded vessels and covered with one huge heap
of wreck from river and ocean – composed of immense
quantities of wood, dead bodies of animals, and furniture of all
kinds.

Tens of thousands of pounds of damage was caused with
some loss of life and about 3000 persons rendered destitute in
some degree or other. A relief fund was established to help
those in real need and distress. Another fund, a 'medal fund'
was also set up to produce some lasting commemoration of the
efforts of a number of people who had either saved lives or had
prevented serious disaster in some way. "On the Spey, at
Rothes and at Garmouth, the same generous, prompt and
effective spirit was shown, with the same gratifying results.

Several lives were saved, though at the most fearful risk of their brave deliverers ...."; so ran the Committee's Report. The Committee adopted as an appropriate design for the medal a view of the Bridge of Spey "after the destruction of the two northern arches, by which the ruins of this noble structure are seen standing amidst the raging flood, emblematical of the devastation it occasioned, and of the important services intended to be commemorated by the medal".

The 1829 flooding stands unparalleled in a history of flooding in the Highlands. A lesser calamity occurred in 1892. In that year the flood happened in midwinter, when the fields were bare, thus reducing the cost of damage to crops. Even so, the flood waters were sufficient to carry away all kinds of farming equipment, hay stacks, potato clamps, and washed away river banks and nearby roads. Perhaps the most dramatic piece of destruction was the loss of a section of the Highland Railway immediately below Belleville, half way between Kingussie and Kincraig stations. The line was carried on an embankment some ten feet high. The last train to pass to the south just managed to cross over the breached section of the embankment, with the water being so high as to all but extinguish the engine fire. Another train actually left Kingussie for Inverness but was stopped in time by the driver sighting danger signals place on the rails by surfacemen. If this had not happened, the train and its passengers would have taken a death dive. As in the 1829 floods, much damage was done to land and buildings, but no loss of life occurred. Even so, dramatic scenes were witnessed on this occasion:

> From Fochabers to the mouth of the Spey at Garmouth, the river presented in miniature the appearance of an inland sea. The land here is almost level, and the great body of water, as soon as it passed the confined area between the bed rocks west of Fochabers, spread out in both directions, completely covering the extensive area of whins and undergrowth. On to the sea the vast volume of water swept, carrying everything before it, cutting out for itself new channels, filling up old ones, and submerging all objects within its reach. Not since the flood of 1829 was such a vast area

of the surrounding country under flood in this district, and not, probably, since that date had the river presented so picturesque and awe-inspiring a sight. Onward the river rolled with an impetuous fury, the waves dashing and breaking as in a storm at sea, ever and anon striking at the massive supports of the bridge, which, standing firm as a rock, resisted the aggression with apparent ease. It was a grand sight to watch from the gigantic structure the seething, eddying mass of water rushing underneath with the roar of a mighty cataract, angry in mood, as it were, because science had rendered the viaduct invincible against its terrible power.

The River Spey still presents a constant danger from flooding, though measures have been taken to ensure that any damage caused by flooding is minimized. In 1977 there was seen the completion of the new mouth cut for the Spey at Kingston. This new mouth was cut to reduce the risk of future flooding and to prevent further erosion and build-up of shingle in the area. The cutting was made about a half-mile to the east of the former river mouth. Thus the unruly Spey is being tamed. One of the most vulnerable parts of the Spey river banks is that great extent of meadow land below Kingussie. In the past this tract became a temporary lake sometimes over six miles in length which at times threatened the stability of the railway line running close by. Dykes were erected in the most vulnerable places, but the underlying surface of water still presents a problem at times, and the land is often wet and marshy. Loch Insh is merely a remnant of the old lake which at one time extended all the way from Kingussie.

As might be expected in an area which varies in height from sea-level to more than 4000 feet above that, the climate can vary considerably, but tends towards a continental type within the general British pattern. There are, however, possibilities of micro-climates created by the massive areas which are covered with trees; a forest can be bathed in mist while outside its perimeters the sun shines on a different scene. The weather can change dramatically in the high range of the Cairngorms. What is often good weather for hill-walking or climbing on the floor of the Spey valley can be quite different once an elevation of 3000 feet is reached, with the possibility of meeting gales and sleet. In winter, when dry snow is lifted off the ground by the wind, 'white-out' conditions are common, when one's feet are quite invisible and one loses all sense of direction. The changes in the weather conditions on the higher slopes are often frequent and confusing, especially if one relies solely on general weather conditions as predicted on the radio. Local forecasts are always the best guide and are available to visitors to the mountains who wish to experience the exhilaration of the high peaks. Needless to say, it is foolhardy to tackle anything but a low-level walk in ordinary clothing. Both accidents and deaths have occurred when people have gone on long high-level treks clad in clothing more suited for shopping in a multiple store. Electrical storms are particularly dangerous on the peaks. All over the Cairngorms range there can be seen evidence of lightning strikes which have broken up surface rocks. On the valley floor, weather conditions tend to approximate to the Moray Firth area, which is dry and mild all year round. However, low temperatures do occur. In 1961 it was found that the soil at Aviemore froze to a depth of two feet, compared with the few inches in normal winter conditions. The Cairngorms area is the snowiest part of the British Isles, and even on the lower slopes snow can be seen well on into the year. On the summits it has been estimated that snow falls on about 100 days each year, and tends to lie in corries out of reach of the sun's rays for most if not all of each year. It is this fact which has been commercialized to provide snow-sport facilities which now all but rival those of the European Alps.

## II

## FOREST, GLEN AND BEN

THE LAND on both sides of the River Spey, as it makes its way from source to mouth, from the drowned lands of Badenoch to the high peaks of the Cairngorms and the Monadhliaths, offers a range of habitats for flora and fauna which is, in many respects, quite unique in the British Isles, if not in Europe. To say that about the area is not simply a sweeping statement, but is an undoubted fact which has emerged from decades of close study by naturalists with both broad and specialist interests. Certainly, the area encompassing the Spey valley offers such a spectrum of species for close study and for casual observation, that it is not surprising that fears are now being expressed for the safety and continued existence of nature in its raw states, as the result of tourist pressures emanating from the developments in that direction in recent years: what was wilderness little more than a decade ago is now becoming accessible to large numbers of people wishing simply to see the grandeur of the wild.

If one hand-crafted and magnificent species sums up the natural gifts of the Spey valley it is the osprey, an example both of man's attitude to wild life, on the one hand heedless of consequences and, on the other, his change of heart and attitude in the light of new knowledge and the appreciation of the fact that all living things contribute to the balance of a scheme of things in which man is but a complementary element. It is a sign of sanity that many people now involved in the conservation of wild life, even though they might offer only token support in a subscription to a conservation organiz-

26

ation, perhaps a decade ago would not have done much else than show or share passive concern. It was the nineteenth-century visionary and mystic poet, Francis Thompson, who said: "Thou cans't not stirr a flower without troubling of a star". That statement, far in advance of its time, contains the idea that all living things on earth share the common experience of life and that the fate of one entity can impinge on the consciousness of others. While the gift of mental association with other persons and living things might be too deep-sunk in the subconscious of many, there are not a few who still display this gift in such experiences as telepathy and precognition. But for the most of us, it is sufficient that we be aware of the intrinsic values of wild life.

Human societies in close contact with nature have always been the most aware of the need to conserve, and to live within an environment circumscribed by local resources and opportunities. One of the perfect examples of this is seen in the approach to life of the American Indian, as written in 1835 by Chief Seathl of the Swamish tribe, in a letter to the President of the United States:

> How can you buy or sell the sky – the warmth of the land? The idea is strange to us. Every shining pine needle, every sandy shore, every mist in the dark woods, every clearing and humming insect is holy in the memory and the experience of my people . . . . The air is precious to the red man. For all things share the same breath – the beasts, the trees, man . . . . The white man must treat the beasts of this land as his brothers. I am a savage and do not understand any other way. I have seen a thousand rotting buffaloes on the prairie, left by the white man who shot them from a passing train. I am a savage and do not understand . . . What is man without the beasts? If all the beasts were gone, man would die from loneliness of spirit, for whatever happens to the beasts also happens to man. All things are connected . . . .

The osprey has rightly been chosen as a symbol of the Spey valley, for its comeback in recent years almost underlines the increased awareness of the very species which reduced its number in the Highlands to the point of extinction many years ago. This comeback was no easy return, for time and time again the birds were frustrated in their nesting by vandals and, worse, egg-collectors. This fish-eating hawk was once common in the Highlands and attracted the attention of many people with double standards. One such was Charles St John. In his *Tour in Sutherlandshire* he writes: "I walked on to look at the osprey's nest in the old castle, and an interesting sight it is, though I lamented the absence of the birds. Why the poor osprey should be persecuted I know not, as it is quite harmless, living wholly on fish, of which everyone knows there is too great an abundance in this country for the most rigid preserver to grudge this picturesque bird his share." From this great show of concern, St John describes, a few pages later, the shooting of a hen osprey and taking two eggs from the nest. Writing of the calling of the distraught male bird he says: "I was really sorry I had shot her", and further tells us of the fate of the male bird: "I am sorry to say that I shot him deliberately in cold blood as he sat". St John is actually on record as shooting the last ospreys in Sutherland on Loch Assynt. Not content with this record, he and a friend were busy for several years in succession in harrying the osprey eyrie in Loch an Eilean, robbing the nest of eggs. It was this locale which Elizabeth Grant described in 1808: "Often the birds rose as we were watching their eyrie, and wheeled skimming over the loch in search of food required by the young eaglets, who could be seen peeping over the pile of sticks that formed their home".

Despite St John's efforts, the osprey returned to the Loch an Eilean site a number of times, but was always the attraction for egg collectors. The year 1899 saw the last attempt by the bird to nest and breed successfully; the greed of the human species had proved too much. In sum, of 26 known nests of the bird, between 1848 and 1902, collectors robbed 14. After 1899 the osprey was extinct insofar as the Highlands were concerned, generally speaking, though the occasional sighting was made; but whether of breeding birds or birds on their migration to the south is not recorded. In 1936 Desmond Nethersole-Thompson, a first-class naturalist of Highland fame, saw single ospreys flying over lochs in Strathspey, but he found no evidence of breeding. Thereafter, the bird was seen at regular intervals until 1954 when a nest was found and its location kept a tight secret. In the following year, a pair was sighted building a nest close to Loch Garten. For nearly twenty years now ospreys have returned from their winter quarters in Africa to nest at Loch Garten under the protection of the Royal Society for the Protection of Birds (RSPB), and, indeed, under whose wing, as it were, they have bred successfully to begin the recolonization of the Highlands with their species. The Loch Garten area of 670 acres around the eyrie was designated an official bird sanctuary initially and the area (now extended to 1517 acres) is now a Reserve purchased by the RSPB in 1975 at a cost of £290,000, the sum mainly representing the value of the unfelled trees in the area.

But life is still difficult for the osprey. The year 1977 saw a decline in the osprey population: down to 12 young birds bred in Scotland compared with 20 the year before, this mainly due to natural factors and the depredations of man. Early in May 1977 a clutch of four eggs, the largest number in a single nest reported this century, was stolen from an eyrie in the Spey valley. Then a raging forest fire swept through 150 acres of forest and heather. A careful watch is now kept on the Loch Garten eyrie, with additional anti-theft devices such as flood-lights, alarm bells and electronic detectors being provided, in each period of 24 hours.

In 1972 two young north-country men were convicted for robbing the Loch Garten eyrie at night. Some colonizing ospreys have been shot by gamekeepers. But the success which has attended the RSPB operation is now seen in the fact that the population is now fourteen breeding pairs. The story of the Speyside ospreys has been recounted worldwide as an example of imaginative nature conservation and interpretation. The birds at Loch Garten feed almost exclusively on fish, mostly trout and pike. It plunges into the water to catch prey with its talons, which are specially designed to grip the wriggling fish. Throughout the breeding season the male supplies the food.

With a wing span of up to five feet, the flying osprey is one of
the magnificent wonders of Speyside, rivalled only by the
golden eagle.

Between the Monadhliath Mountains and the Cairngorm
range there is now a near-static resident population of golden
eagles, members of which can often be seen soaring like moving
punctuation marks against the skyline. The bird is specially
protected under the Protection of Birds Act, 1954, but is still
often killed illegally in remote hill country and its nests are
robbed. A pair of breeding eagles requires between 4000 and
18,000 acres to sustain them, one reason why the bird, if seen, is
usually a solitary winger. The main complaint against the eagle
is that it kills lambs and grouse. While the lamb may be part of
the diet in such places as Wester Ross, where game is scarce, it
is not a preferred food, as has been noted in the Eastern
Highlands where the diet is more often than not rabbit or
mountain hare, or deer carrion. The eyries of the eagle are a
great attraction to egg collectors who rob the eggs, often with
the help of gamekeepers. Stories abound among ornithologists
of attempts by collectors who go to great and often absurd
lengths to deprive mating pairs of their eggs. The main
importance of the Cairngorm eagles is that they represent a
reservoir of reasonably healthy stock, uncontaminated by
organo-chlorine pesticides which is often the fate of eagles in
other areas, and which could be used to stock new ground or
lost territories.

Another bird of hill and ben in Strathspey is the snowy owl.
This bird is more at home in high-arctic tundra, but has been
seen in the Cairngorms, more frequently in recent years. The
bird has now bred successfully on Fetlar, in Shetland, and
moves south on occasions to winter and summer on a moor in
lower Speyside. Larger than buzzards, they fly over snow fields
searching for their favourite food, voles and ptarmigan. There
are hopes that a pair might start to breed in the area, to add
another 'first' to Speyside's credit.

The snow-bunting is one of the rarest of Scottish birds. In
the last hundred years, hunters have found less than fifty nests

with eggs in the Cairngorm hills. In historic times only a few pairs have been known to nest in the Cairngorms, but it has been suggested that decades of severe winters in Iceland and in Scandinavia will chase this migrant to Scotland's high hills to become a permanent settler in larger numbers than in recent years.

Other hill birds in Speyside include the dotterel, now making a comeback to recolonize a few lower hills in the Grampians, and the ptarmigan, usually found wherever crow-berry or blueberry are abundant (on ground with boulders or screes). You must climb high to see these birds, to at least 2000 feet. The ptarmigan was a popular 'shoot' in Victorian times, when it was fashionable to go out on wholesale-slaughter expeditions. Nowadays, it is the honest and innocent tourist who represents the greatest danger to the ptarmigan, by damaging or destroying vegetation on the hills with fragile areas. Even so, the species manages to keep its numbers up, even on the disturbed habitats near the ski-lifts of Coire Cas and Cairnwell.

The dotterel is among the most beautiful of the hill birds in the high Cairngorms. They have deep chocolate crowns, white cheeks and eye-stripes which meet at the nape; a broad white crescent separates the brown of the upper and lower chest and flank. They were first noted hereabouts in 1769, when Thomas Pennant was touring the Highlands. In 1786 the extrovert sportsman, Colonel Thornton, killed a dotterel using a tiercel and he shot another. In more recent times the bird has begun to recolonize a few of the lower hills in the Grampians, and this fact presents a danger to the population, for the birds are quite tame and are easy prey and playthings for tourists' dogs not on the leash. They are not numerous, but add a charming vignette to the Cairngorm scene above the 3000 foot levels.

Animals in Speyside are more readily seen and spotted. Perhaps one of the most interesting is a foreigner, yet was once a native of Scotland: the reindeer. Caithness is supposed to have been the last place in Scotland where the species survived until the twelfth century. There is a tradition that the Jarls of

Orkney, in the tenth century, were in the habit of crossing the Pentland Firth to hunt the reindeer in the wilds of Caithness. The species was familiar to ancient man. A reindeer appears on a carved stone of the early Christian period, found at Grantown-on-Spey, indicating that the recently introduced animal was at one time no stranger to Speyside and the Cairngorms. Last century, various attempts were made to re-introduce the species to Scotland, but they all met with failure. In 1952 some mountain and forest reindeer, all of domesticated stock, were introduced to Glenmore from Lapland, sponsored by the British Reindeer Company, under the guidance of Mikel Utsi, a Lapp from northern Sweden. The company settled a small herd inside a fenced enclosure on forest marsh near Moor Bing. Later, the animals were herded in an area south of Loch Morlich, enclosing old pine forest and windswept moorland. The object of the experiment was to find out whether the animals could be satisfactorily established on a commercial basis, without any addition to the staple diet of reindeer moss. In summer the animals now roam on the Ben Macdhui plateau and Carn Lochain. The herd has slowly built up and now numbers one hundred, all Scottish-born animals. They can be seen near the ski grounds. Tourists are advised not to feed scraps to them, or let untrained dogs chase them. The deer have suffered losses in the past from accidents and, more sinister, poaching.

Other animals of the Spey valley and its high slopes include roe deer, red deer, mountain hare, common shrew, weasel and mink - the latter escapees from captivity where they were bred for furs in Glen Livet until 1965. Since then increasing numbers have been killed along the rivers, but they are still spreading fast. They are cruel and vicious animals, now that the spreading populations are in a feral state. The fox maintains a steady population and is to be seen all over the Cairngorms. Even in deep midwinter, their tracks can be seen in the snow crossing from one corrie to another.

Large herds of roe deer can be seen in Rothiemurchus; the small fields at Inverdruie are rich feeding grounds for them.

A stream flows into the River Spey a few miles from its source at Melgarve.

Two bridges over the young Spey: (*above*) at Melgarve and (*below*) Garva Bridge.

The river near Garva Bridge and (*below*) at Laggan.

Looking over the river towards Kingussie.

Newtonmore

Two popular images of Scotland: (*above*) a piper crosses the Spey at Kincraig Bridge and (*below*) a stag in the snow, at the Highland Wildlife Park at Kincraig.

Inshriach Farm between Feshiebridge and Aviemore and (*below*) Rothiemurchus.

Two Speyside lochs: Loch-an-Eilan and (*below*) Loch Morlich with the Cairngorms in the distance.

Regarded as a pest by foresters because they eat young trees and destroy many trees in summer by fraying the bark with their antlers, they do add a degree of interest to the area to reinforce the variety of wild life seen in the Spey valley. The red deer often raid farms without the protection of deer fences, and they play havoc with turnip, oats, rape and other crops. Even so, they, too, present the visitor with a magnificent taste of the wildlife, seen against the background of a hillside or against the delicious trees they long for.

One animal which never fails to excite interest is the wild goat. Although feral goats disappeared from the Cairngorms earlier this century, a group now lives on the rocks near Carr Bridge. The original animals existed in what is now Glenmore National Park. But one wild winter, an avalanche struck the herd and completely destroyed it, with no survivors. The present population in parts of the Spey valley came into the limelight a year or so back when a row flared up in the Press over the shooting of wild goats on a Speyside estate. They do, in fact, present something of a problem. They breed rapidly and, in the absence of natural predators, can quickly destroy all kinds of plant life and all too soon find themselves in a goat-created desert. The herd on Creagdhu, between New-tonmore and Laggan, are reasonably tame. The shooting incident was the result of an effort by the estate-owner who became concerned at the destruction by the goats of young trees and valuable grazing at the expense of his sheep stock. Goat-trophy hunting was offered and taken up by hunters; the going rate for a week's shooting is £600 or so. The concern of the conservationists is based on the fact that much of the Highland landscape is fragile and cannot stand the overgrazing which is the hallmark of unmanaged goat herds. The present Creagdhu herd was established some years ago by the pro-prietor of old Cluny Castle, who had the animals brought over from Islay, the object being to displace sheep from grazing the dangerous cliff. Though their numbers were reduced to twelve one very severe winter, they have since increased and now tend to wander to more attractive pastures; though at breeding times they return to their native rocks. The argument about the position of wild goats will always go on, generating more heat than light. Perhaps if some way can be devised to control their movements, they could become an acceptable (to foresters and farmers) part of the natural wild life of the valley.

Now to the waters. The River Spey and its tributaries, and the valley's lochs, have always been noted for their fish populations, trout and salmon in particular. Access to these waters has, however, always been in dispute and recent legal battles have produced gains and concessions as well as losses. Salmon fishing was a communal sport until about 1850; the fish provided food for the farm labourer and it was caught by lights, nets and pronged forks. The later years of last century saw the 'sporting' types flocking into the Highlands for some diversification and the salmon became overnight the guarded property of estate owners and a status sport for the wealthy. Fishing by forks became illegal in 1868. The local people then reverted to poaching, using nets, gaffs (hooks snatched through the water), and the illegal bait of salmon eggs. These methods are still used.

To the devoted and enthusiastic angler, the Spey in particular offers excellent sport, though in recent years the sea stock of salmon has been so depleted by factory fishing outside British territorial sea limits that the fish is not now so plentiful as it was. The Atlantic salmon swim up river from the sea from October onwards. In some mild winters when there are periods of high water, they can be found as far up the Spey as Aviemore; in most years, however, they tend to stay in the lower reaches nearer the mouth, which is why beats on the river there have the best early fishing. The fish spawn during October and November in gravel redds or nests, usually in the larger tributaries and in small streams. The fish are good climbers and salmon have been known to spawn well past Laggan on the Spey, and have also been seen at heights of over 1800 feet above sea level, up the Tromie, the Avon and the Feshie rivers. The selling and letting of salmon fishing rights involves fantastic sums these days. In 1966, a stretch along one bank of the River Dee, just over a mile in length, fetched £68,000.

Although sea trout often smaller than salmon, some fish weighing over 20 lb have been caught in the rivers of the Cairngorms. Most sea trout enter fresh water in summer and make for the tributaries which drain the middle and lower reaches of the Spey watershed. Brown trout are very widespread in lochs and streams, and are also found in the main rivers. These fish are resident in the fresh waters and never go to sea. They spawn in gravel redds like the salmon. They can be found in streams as high as 2500 feet above sea level and have even been caught occasionally in small steep fast-running streams at 2800 feet. They are the favourite food for the osprey, and fish farms in the Spey valley, such as that at Inverdruie, have suffered significant losses from the birds. There are a number of angling courses offered in the Spey valley, to introduce the sport to newcomers and to help veterans improve their fishing and casting techniques. In all the courses, the emphasis is on casting proficiency rather than the taking of fish – the first, however, usually leads to the second. Other fish which are to be found in the waters feeding into Strathspey include char and pike.

One of the problems which has increased in stature over the years concerns that of access to rivers by the general public. The law was, until recently, quite vague about the rights of free access to waters, not just for fishing, but for the use of river waters for sailing from one part to another, even crossing from one river bank to another. The matter came to a head in 1972 when Clive Freshwater won a notable and significant battle involving the right to use a river for the passage of a canoe. Mr Freshwater had set up his own canoeing and sailing school in 1969 on Loch Insh, through which flows the Spey. Early in 1972 his small company, the Cairngorm Canoeing and Sailing School Ltd, was served with a writ taken out against him on behalf of the Trustees of the Knockando Estate. The writ sought to prevent him from taking his canoes on the water which passed through the estate because it was alleged this interfered with the salmon fishing. At the time he never realized that his case would eventually reach the House of Lords, to be debated by some of the finest legal brains in the country, including Lords Hailsham and Dilhorne. These men searched back into Roman and Napoleonic law which had, in 1782, pronounced on a case between the Duke of Gordon and various members of the Clan Grant. The 1782 case was vital because it was held to have established a public right of navigation on the Spey with the vessels consisting, at that time, of rafts of timber steered by a man with an oar. The Law Lords ruled by a majority of four to one that the Duke of Gordon case had decided that the Spey was a public navigable river and that therefore Clive Freshwater could take his canoes down it. Although the judgement related only to Scottish rivers, it will affect future cases of a similar kind; the decision also made the distinction between access to rivers for the purpose of navigation, and access to hills and rights of way over land.

The original case presented by Clive Freshwater took some four years to resolve and cost in excess of £35,000. Even the argument in the House of Lords lasted eight weeks and involved nine Law Lords before the final decision was obtained. The battle was fought in various arenas, including the Edinburgh Court of Sessions, the Appeal Court, and the House of Lords. The case was important because it was seen in the context of the moral position of the land-owning class in the British Isles. There are about 55 million acres in Britain and 56 million people. But some people own many thousands of acres; in the Highlands of Scotland, less than 300 families own more than 5 million acres of land, which is over nine percent of the land surface of Britain. Much of this land is owned because the ancestors of those families were granted it in reward for services rendered to the Crown of the day – a practice that has long ceased in Britain. Nowadays, some of these families – an increasing number – take a modern and enlightened view of their land possessions. They regard themselves as custodians of the land on behalf of those who live and work on it, and on behalf of the nation. Voluntarily they allow access to their land

and waters on very similar grounds to those granted by law in the high peaks: basically, that each group should respect the interests of the other. The argument on the Spey rights was that however much one side respected the other's interests, there was no way they could live together: that canoeing and fishing in the same stretch of water were incompatible. Indeed, the original judge involved in the case, Lord Maxwell, came to the conclusion that canoeing did indeed have an effect on fishing which was "more than minimal"; but he also stated that he could not define it more accurately than that. The case raised by Mr Freshwater was also seen in a social context and, at one time, could have become political, because some political parties are intent on passing land into some form of public ownership varying from out-and-out nationalization to community control.

The case highlighted three important facets of land and water rights. First, that there is only a limited amount of recreational land and water that cannot be claimed by one person or group for their exclusive use. Secondly, that all who use the land or water must respect it, and have regard for those who make their living from it and for those who use it for other recreational purposes. Thirdly, that most of the land must remain undeveloped, otherwise it ceases to have any value as a fresh-air lung for the nation.

Offering as it does a unique environment for all species of wild life, the Spey valley contains much of interest to the botanist, the geologist, and the ornithologist, and also, in some respects, acts as a natural free-roaming museum of some rare species. The rare crested tit, found nowhere else in the British Isles, favours only the shelter of the Spey valley woodlands, and is typical of the concern of conservationists, when they view the increasing pressures being created in fragile habitats. One example was the suggestion in 1977 that a desolate stretch of moorland, at Braeval Wood about three miles from Carr Bridge, should be used as a dumping ground for chemical and other industrial wastes, including arsenic and cyanide, oil, grease, sludge tar and bitumen. Many consider this would be in effect a chemical time-bomb, in that the gradual seepage of these materials into the ground would eventually pollute the Spey river system. The faceless planners may well meet organized opposition to this suggestion when more details have been released. Towards the end of 1977 plans were announced for the creation of a long-distance route, to be called the Speyside Way, running from the Spey Bay area to Glenmore, along the disused railway tracks, primarily so that tourists could motor through areas of scenic beauty and interest, with additional proposals for branch pedestrian routes from Nethybridge, via Boat of Garten, to Aviemore. These and other 'plans' are coming under the scrutiny of the energetic Badenoch and Strathspey Conservation Group who act as public watchdogs. The proposal for the creation of 'special' ways, for instance was opposed because a path system already exists from Nethybridge to Aviemore; and there was a strong case for the creation of a better network of paths rather than a special tourist road facility. As the Group said in a statement, it was a mistake ". . . to positively encourage more people going this way since Glenmore is already under heavy pressure and cannot stand much more without irreparable damage". The Group's alternative suggestion was to terminate the proposed way at Aviemore.

Just how significant the Spey valley is as a winter playground area is seen in the rated capacity on Cairngorm of 9000 skiers, with recent proposals for development to add another 6000 skiers in the area of Lurcher's Gully and two neighbouring corries. Little wonder then that continued expansion is being looked at closely and with some concern for the introduction of controlling techniques if the area is not to be completely despoiled.

While it is accepted that these are more enlightened times, the intrusion of man into any area must be seen in the context of the past, and particularly in the fate of some of the animal species which were once native to Scotland but are now extinct. The improvement of the climate after the last glaciation in Scotland extinguished such mammals as the mammoth, woolly rhinoceros, musk ox, cave bear, giant fallow, arctic fox and the lemming. The red deer of Pleistocene times were replaced by the smaller forms of the present day. The elk, reindeer, wild cat, bison, brown bear, wolf and beaver survived into historic times. The bison and wild cattle were probably the first to disappear in the early Iron Age. The bear may well have existed until the tenth century; the reindeer and elk a little longer – there were reports of beavers in Inverness-shire in the sixteenth century. The mammal fauna of the Cairngorms, in particular, was once very rich. Indeed, it has been suggested on slender evidence that elk, brown bear and wild ox survived in the region until the ninth or tenth centuries, and wild boars until the early seventeenth century. These animals have now disappeared.

An attractive theory of the late T. C. Lethbridge, an archaeologist of enquiring mind and so unorthodox in his methods that he was often frowned upon by his professional colleagues, suggested that many Scottish clans are descended from Celtic tribes who were often named after animals. For example, the Chatti (cats) of Rhineland may be, at the present time, reflected in the Clan Chattan, the cat clan, to which belong the Macphersons, the Mackintoshes, and Shaws, all of whom bear a cat in their coats of arms. Are they the modern equivalent of the old Cats of War, the Cattubellauni? The association of many Highland clans with their country's native animals, extinct and rare, is possibly much older than we suspect.

The European bear was once a common animal in the old Caledonian forests. Bishop Leslie tells us that this great woodland was once "refertissima", full of them. Camden, another writer of old, says: "This Athole is a country fruitful enough, having wood vallies, where once the Caledonian Forest (dreadful for its dark intricate windings and for its dens of bears) extended itself far and near in these parts." Camden also quotes Plutarch in saying that Scottish bears were transported to Rome " ... where they held them in great admiration". During the Roman occupation of Britain, Caledonian bears were well known in Rome for their exceptional beauty and size, and they were prized as one of the animals able to provide bloody spectacles in the Coliseum and other Roman amphitheatres. A number of Gaelic-based place-names in the Highlands indicate that the bear was commonly known.

The wild boar was one of the oldest animals in the British Isles and is the one which has the earliest mention in history. The Gordon family, which eventually came to own much of Speyside, was given the right to sport three boars' heads on their banners: the result of an ancestor who, about 1057, had killed a fierce boar in the Forest of Huntly. The wolf, too, was once common in Scotland, so much so that it was necessary to erect refuges for the safety of travellers overtaken by night, for fear of an attack by the animal. These refuges were called Spitals, a name which occurs in, for example, the Spittal of Glenshee, on the Devil's Elbow road from Blairgowrie to Braemar. One of the last wolves to be killed in Scotland was a beast which breathed its last at the hands of a stalker to the Mackintosh, named MacQueen, who dispatched the animal near the River Findhorn in 1743.

The fate of many of the now-extinct animals was often a result of their direct links with man who, for various reasons, found himself unable to live in their presence. Often regarded as vermin, fit for nothing but sport, they were hunted and killed in great numbers. Many recorded instances tell of organized hunts which ended in wholesale slaughter. While it can be argued that the wolf, for instance, was a real danger to the human species in Scotland, it is perhaps a cause for regret that a true native of the Highland wilderness had to be weighed in the balance and found wanting, thereby removing an interesting specimen from the natural museum which the Highlands have always offered extinct, rare and threatened species. But that is an argument which could carry on to the wee sma' hours over a good malt whisky from Speyside. Some small but significant act of reparation is seen at Kincraig, at the Highland Wildlife Park, where many of the rare animals, once indigenous to the Spey valley and the Cairngorms, are now kept in a free-roaming environment, and where, too, are to be seen some examples, brought from other places in the world, of now-extinct Highland animals. Viewing these, one tends to appreciate all the more the efforts of those who are now trying to bring back some of the things which man has lost without pangs of regret, but which somehow still remain on his conscience.

# III

## FROM SOURCE TO MOUTH

THE SPEY is the second longest river in Scotland. The source of its 98 mile journey is Loch Spey, which lies some 1143 feet above sea level on the border marches between Badenoch and Lochaber, both areas so redolent of Highland history that they seem to have passed on its atmosphere to the river which, among few such in Scotland, has created for itself a niche in the affairs of the country at large. It has been described as the most rapid river in Scotland. It makes a respectable 'fall' in its first few miles until it reaches the flat lands around Kingussie; then, collecting waters from turbulent tributaries, it tumbles along at a rate which continues apace until the mouth is reached at Kingston, where even the strength of the sea tides is not able to force seawater upstream for much more than half a mile. Loch Spey is fed mainly by streams from the slopes of Creag a' Bhanain, with an outflow of water which belies the nature of the young river in its journey to the Moray Firth coastline. The river lives up to its name of being the most rapid of all rivers of its size in Britain. Its average fall from Loch Spey to its mouth is 11½ feet per mile, compared with, for example, under 2 feet in the case of the River Thames. In addition, unlike most rivers which tend to flow gently into the sea, the Spey increases the pace in its journey from source to mouth, a fact which creates problems when both sea and river waters meet, particularly when the river is in full flood and a good gale is blowing from the north-east.

The Spey meets up with human history less than five miles from its source when it merges with the waters of Allt Yairack, flowing from the Corrieyairack Pass, at Melgarve. There are many passes in Scotland, those cossetted depressions in a geological grammar which play so many important roles in the history of human settlements. Some are famous: Glencoe and Killiecrankie conjure up a vivid pageantry with little effort. Some others are, however, equally well deserving of fame, but are often kept in the obscure light of the public eye by their very inaccessibility. The Corrieyairack Pass carries a road built by General Wade in 1732, running from Cullachy, just south of Fort Augustus on Loch Ness, to Dalwhinnie at the head of another pass, the Drumochter; much of the route of this road follows the young River Spey as it flows towards Newton-more. The road was built primarily to allow the easy shift of Government troops between the barracks then being con-structed in the Highlands. The period which followed the 1715 Rising was one of considerable unrest in the Highlands. The Disarming Act of 1719 only served to increase the feeling of bitterness among the Highland clans. Lord Lovat, for one, among other well-known and prominent Highland chiefs, insisted that the Government take steps to stop further dis-affection and disloyalty.

Thus, on 23rd July 1724, Major-General Wade was in-structed to proceed to the Highland and report on Lord Lovat's Memorial. In December of that year Wade received his commission as Commander-in-Chief of the forces in North Britain. Among Wade's recommendations for "reducing the Highlands to obedience" he stated that money would be required "for the mending of roads between garrisons and barracks for the better communication of His Majesty's Troops". By the end of 1725 Wade had begun the construction of his great military highway through the Great Glen, from Fort William to Inverness. This was followed by the building of the road southwards from Inverness to Dunkeld, in Perth-shire. In 1731 he commenced the building of a road from Fort Augustus over Corrieyairack to Dalwhinnie and Dalnacardoch, thence by Trinafour and Tummel to Aberfeldy and Crieff. These constituted the three main lines of communication built by Wade between 1725 and 1733, a period of eight years during which, with some minor connections, he constructed a total of 250 miles of roadway. Relieved of his command in 1740, Wade lived to the ripe old age of 75 and was buried in 1748 in Westminster Abbey.

Building the Corrieyairack road was no easy task. Some 500 men were employed on the project. Masons and skilled men were paid 1s 6d per day for bridge-building, and horse-labour 5s a day for cart and two horses. The rough-work was carried out by military parties under the command of their own officers, extra pay being allowed the men for the really tough conditions they encountered. The construction of the road up to the south face of the Corrieyairack by a series of seventeen traverses was the most difficult part of the construction undertaken by Wade's troops. Later, the number of traverses was reduced to thirteen. Robert Chambers describes the traverses: ". . . each of which leads the traveller but a small way forward in the actual course of his journey. A stone buttress some ten to fifteen feet in height retains each traverse on its outward side; while a drain or water-course was constructed on the inward side." Another impressive feature of the road was the double-arched bridge spanning the Spey at Garvamore. It was named 'St George's Bridge', after George II. It is a handsome structure of two arches, each of forty feet span, joining the centre pier which stands on solid load-bearing rock in the middle of the river.

The road ran for some 22 miles and was completed in about six months. The statistics indicate that it was finished at the rate of one yard per man per day, a feat which is impressive even in terms of the sophisticated techniques available to road-builders in these modern times. The spring of 1732 saw the road in full use for wheeled vehicles and the transport of troops and artillery. Wade himself drove over it with his officers in a carriage drawn by six horses; it is said that his appearance on the summit (2,922 feet above sea level before it falls steeply through the watershed of the River Tarff) caused no end of consternation among the Highland hill folk who witnessed the incident. The total cost was in the region of £3300 for "... carrying on the New Road or Wheel Carriage from the New Fortress of Fort Augustus to joyn the great Road made in the Preceding Years from Crieff to Inverness, and for Building Stone Bridges where they should be found necessary".

At first Wade's roads were resented, not unnaturally. They represented easy access to the hitherto inaccessible tracts of land owned by Highland chiefs who claimed that the coming of strangers among them threatened to "... destroy or weaken that attachment of their vassals, which it is so necessary for them to support and preserve".

Edward Burt wrote:

> The middling order say the roads are to them an inconvenience instead of being useful, as they have turned them out of their old ways; for their horses being never shod, the gravel would soon whet away their hoofs, so as to render them unserviceable; whereas the rocks and moor-stones, though together they make a rough way, yet considered separately, they are generally pretty smooth on the surface where they tread .... The lowest class, who many of them at some times cannot compass a pair of shoes for themselves, allege that the gravel is intolerable for their naked feet; and the complaint has extended to their thin brogues. It is true they do sometimes for these reasons go without the road, and ride or walk in very incommodious ways.

If the new roads were intolerable, the bridges were even more so. The chiefs held that the provision of bridges across rivers and turbulent streams would make the people effeminate, and incapable of crossing other rivers and streams without artificial aids. Indeed, progress has ever had a hard time of it to make itself acceptable.

In time the road became accepted by travellers, drovers and others. However, long before General Wade decided on the Corrieyairack Pass as a suitable connecting route, it was used by the drovers of the great herds of Highland cattle, who took them from the west coast of Scotland to the cattle trysts of Crieff and Falkirk. The cattle were collected from places as far away as Skye (the cattle had to swim across the Sound of Sleat at Kylerhea) and driven to Fort Augustus through the Pass of Corrieyairack to forgather at the Pitmain Bridge over the Spey, for payment of tolls before moving south through the Pass of Drumochter. Droves from this route met other herds from Inverness and the north at Dalwhinnie. In 1723 an observer found at Dalwhinnie no fewer than eight droves (1200 beasts in all) bound for Crieff, and in the Drumochter Pass a drove a mile long, with 300 more cattle resting at the head of Loch Garry. When Wade built his road through the Corrieyairack Pass, it was the drovers who objected that the hard core laid down wore the feet of the beasts; often cattle had to be shod to protect them on their long treks. The year 1890 saw the last of herds of horses brought over the pass to the Falkirk Tryst; cattle were driven over it until 1896 and sheep until 1899. Over the years, too, tales of travelling over the road were added to a growing stock to make a record of fascinating reading. Only one description is selected, because it is comprehensive and gives a glimpse into travelling conditions in the eighteenth century.

It concerns the journey undertaken by the Hon. Mrs Murray of Kensington in her book *A Guide to the Beauties of Scotland &c, to which is added a more Particular Description of Scotland, especially that part of it called the Highlands.* She crossed this desolate mountain pass in 1798:

As we were sitting at breakfast with the good Governor of Fort Augustus, an Oxonian sent in his name, begging leave to see the Fort. He had permission, and was invited to breakfast; he was a very genteel young man, and gave us some account of his tour .... At Dalwhinnie the road to Fort Augustus over Corryarraick branches from the great Inverness road. None of this young gentleman's party dared to encounter that road, except himself and servant, on horseback; the rest went on to Inverness by the great road. The day he crossed Corryarraick was a continued violent rain and storm of wind, which gave it the appearance of wild desolation, beyond anything he could describe; and the whole of the road itself, he said, was rough, dangerous, and dreadful, even for a horse. The steep and black mountains, and the roaring torrents, rendered every step his horse took, frightful; and when he attained the summit of the zigzag up Corryarraick, he thought the horses, himself, man and all, would be carried away, he knew not whither; so strong was the blast, so hard the rain, and so very thick the mist; and as for clod, it stupefied him. He thought it almost a miracle to escape unhurt from such horrid wastes, unwholesome vapours, and frightful fogs; drenched from top to toe, frozen with cold, and half dead with fatigue. He said he had heard people had gone that pass in a carriage, but he was sure it was impossible. The governor's family assured him that it was done frequently; and turning to me, said "here is one who means to do so tomorrow, in a chaise". The gentleman stared, and added, "Then I must alter my journal, for I thought it impossible". A young lady present said she had crossed the mountain on horseback in winter, when snow was on the ground, but it was hazardous. Many, by imprudence, have there lost their lives in winter; particularly some poor woman, attending on a marching troop, carrying an infant in her arms. At the top of the mountain she sank, and would not be persuaded to be removed, nor suffer the child to be taken from her .... The woman and child were later found dead.

Mrs Murray and her party prepared for the adventure the following day, leaving Fort Augustus at eight in the morning. When she reached the summit of the pass she studied her surroundings:

It was certainly cold enough for my great coat; but I became neither torpid nor frozen. I discharged my plough horses .... When I came to the beginning of the zigzag, the sun began to shine; and to the south-west, above the rest of the mountain ocean's waves, I saw Ben Nivis, which I distinguished from the other mountains, it being rendered conspicuous by the sun shining upon its white patches of snow. At the commencement of the zigzag I got out of the carriage, and walked down at my leisure; amusing myself by picking up curious stones and pebbles in the channels made by the torrents, which cross the road at every five or ten yards. Round the base of the mountain, at some distance from the zigzag, is a stream, into which other torrents dash; leaving behind them broad channels of smooth stones, washed from the higher parts. The road is so cut up by these torrents, from the top of the zigzag to the entrance of the plain, that for four or five miles scarcely ten yards can be found free of them; which is, indeed, sufficient to pull a light carriage to pieces. Allen led the horses, and the wheels being dragged, he came quietly and safely to the bottom of that extraordinary pass . . . .

Perhaps the most famous traverse of the pass and Wade's road was made by the troops of the Forty-five Rising under Prince Charlie. The Commander-in-Chief of the Government's forces at the time was General Sir John Cope. On 2nd July 1745 he reported to the Marquis of Tweeddale, who was then Secretary for Scotland, that a strong rumour was circulating to the effect that Prince Charles had arrived in the Highlands. Cope was sceptical of this, but took the precaution of advising Tweeddale that various Highland forts should be supplied with arms and ammunition. Eventually the Government became nervous and ordered Cope to take an army into the Highlands to nip the rebellion in the bud. Cope was unable to handle a situation bound in as it was by rumour and had to be persuaded, by Jacobite sympathizers, it is said, to march northwards. The advance began on 20th August under difficult circumstances:

> The Royal army was not only inferior in numbers to that which Charles was believed to have drawn together, but had all the disadvantages of a campaign in an enemy's country, and on ground unsuitable for its evolutions. It would first have to drag its way slowly over rugged wilderness, with a perpetual clog of .baggage and provisions behind it, and then perhaps fight in a defile where it would be gradually cut to pieces, or what was as bad, permit the enemy to slip past and descend upon the Low Country, which it ought to have protected, [so wrote Robert Chambers in his *History of the Rebellion in Scotland.*]

Cope in fact decided to march into Fort Augustus, over the recently constructed road in the Corrieyairack Pass, a route which would have given him a direct confrontation with the Jacobite army. Indeed, when news came to Prince Charlie that Cope's forces were encamped at Garbhamore on the eastern end of the pass, he was thrilled: "Before I take off these

broguews," he remarked, "I shall engage with Mr Cope!"
General Cope was, however, beset with problems. His own
forces were in no condition to face a fierce and bloody battle,
particularly as information came to him that the Highlanders
were entrenched in the pass and that there would be no hope of
him breaking through to gain Fort Augustus – alive, let alone
wounded. So he reluctantly decided to head north for Inverness, after full consultation with his officers who agreed, to a
man, that as the Government's instructions were explicit in his
going north, it would lead to criticism if he did not do so.
There was also the morale of his men to consider. According to
a local tradition recorded by the Rev. Donald Cameron,
Laggan's shinty-hating minister, Cope " ... took a simple
method to try the firmness of their nerves. Pointing to a clump
of wood about two miles distant, he exclaimed 'Yonder are the
Highlanders!' The result evinced that his companions in arms
were, by no means, in a fighting humour; for, it is said, that the
whole seemed to tremble from head to foot." So Cope retreated
from his encampment on the banks of the Spey and headed
north. Not far from Dalcholly House there is a little group of
trees known locally as Cope's Turn, marking the place where
local tradition says he abandoned his intended advance westwards to Fort Augustus. Cope was later to make his own mark
on the pages of Scotland's history with his defeat at Prestonpans
and become the butt of the most famous rebel song of the
whole campaign: "Hey, Johnnie Cope, are ye waukin yet?"

One can still traverse along Wade's old road, though it has
deteriorated considerably in parts. The old bridge has been
damaged by the Spey in spate. Other parts of the route make
for difficult walking, but it can be done in up to five hours.
Wheeled transport have recently gone all the way, but it is a
route for four-wheeled drives rather than the modern low-
slung, pleasure-going cars of today. A broken engine sump or
axle is that last mishap one would seek on this road. But for the
intrepid hill-walker, well-clad and shod, it provides one of the
most interesting scenic vistas the Highlands can offer, particularly from the height of Corrieyairack Hill, from which, at

2922 feet above sea level, one can look back towards Strathspey and the Grampians and, to the west, the Great Glen with mountains and innumerable lochs. For the able, the trek should be a major ambition. There have been suggestions made that the Highland Regional Authority should look at the road to render it fit for pedestrian traffic only, for it is undoubtedly a route of scenic importance, with an exciting history almost every step of the way.

From Melgarve the Spey hurries on over a rocky channel at Garva Bridge, a two-arched structure, well buttressed to take the power of the rushing waters when the river is in flood. Built by General Wade's men, it was formerly known as St George's Bridge; it has stood the test of nearly two and a half centuries. Nearby is Garbhamore (Garvamore), where the remains of the Kingshouse stands, built by Wade to shelter troops as they trekked from one side of Scotland to the other, and to offer some food and shelter at the end of a long day's march. These King's Houses also served civilian travellers. The inn at Garbhamore, while still standing, is fast turning into dereliction. The interior was almost intact until a few years ago; indeed, the house was occupied until shortly before the last war. Prince Charles Edward slept here on his march southwards from Fort Augustus and the building is listed as being of national interest. However, being off the beaten track it is seemingly of no great concern to the authorities that the building is now deteriorating. Two of the old box-beds in the building now repose in the comfort, care and keeping of the West Highland Museum at Fort William. The building was once a school which served the few children in the district.

The buildings at Garbhamore are the property of the British Aluminium Company, who are based at Fort William and Kinlochleven, where they have the aluminium reduction factories. The company also owns part of upper Strathspey along the road leading to the Corrieyairack Pass. Garbhamore was occupied about ten years ago by a shepherd and his family, but was taken out of occupation, along with the old farmstead of Drumin, some miles higher up the strath. The company offered the buildings to the Clan Macpherson Association, and it would have been most encouraging for the clan to have owned a place which had long and historic memories with the Macphersons. But a condition attached to the proposed gift was that the buildings should not be used as a hostel for people walking the Corrieyairack – its original purpose as built by General Wade. After much discussion the gift was refused, for the Association considered that unless the buildings could generate some revenue, the financial burden of upkeep would be too great to bear. Thus, the buildings are left to the attention of weathering, and will no doubt fall into such a ruinous state that nothing could be done to restore them except at great expense.

From Garbhamore, the Spey flows eastwards into an expanse of water dammed at one end by the Spey Dam, overlooking which is the ancient fort of Dun-da-Laimh (the Fort of Two Hands), reckoned to be the most perfect relic of a British stronghold of the Pictish era to be found. Nearby is the site of the old Catholic church of St Michael's Chapel, which was derelict and then blown up in the early 1960s, rather than allow it to be desecrated by vandals. A little to the west of Laggan Bridge begins the series of embankments built to control the flooding of the Spey as it moves into low-lying ground. At Laggan Bridge, in God's Acre of the Church there, lies the remains of Mrs Grant, famous for her *Letters from the Mountains*, as well as for other publications depicting the Highland way of life and living. The flat land between Dalcholly, just below Spey Dam, and before the Spey joins forces with the River Truim, was reckoned be geologists to have been at one time the bed of a loch, now drained by the sluggish waters of the Spey as it meanders through the meadow-land. To the north of the junction of the Spey and the Truim is the long rocky hill known as Creag Dubh (Black Hill), from which the Clan Macpherson derives its war cry. It has a steep front with an irregular outline to the river. To the north of Creag Dubh, at the junction of the A86, from Spean Bridge in Lochaber and the A9 main roadway from Perth to Inverness, stands Newtonmore.

This village, now geared to cater for the tourist industry, houses the Clan Macpherson Association Museum, established just after the last war. The association has been fortunate in being able to lay hands on many of the ancient relics of the clan, and house these in an excellent building which has extended its area with the help of commercial interests and the Highlands & Islands Development Board. But history in Newtonmore is not merely preserved in static objects. The village is vitalized each year with the Newtonmore Games and the Clan Macpherson Rally. The village is also an important centre for the ancient Gaelic-based sport of shinty, a strenuous ball game which demands stamina, skill and courage. Indeed, the area hereabouts is one of the shinty heartlands in the Highlands, along with Skye, Lochaber and north of Inverness. The origins of Newtonmore are obscure, but it is supposed that the first permanent settlers were connected with droving cattle. The low arable ground in the vicinity of the present golf course is where the cattle, after being brought over the Corrieyairack Pass from Lochness-side, were herded together before being taken to the market at Pitmain, near Kingussie.

Kingussie is the capital of Badenoch. A guide book of some fifty years ago insists that because of the pine woods which abound in the vicinity "the air of the place is highly beneficial to sufferers of chest complaints". Certainly, standing at 750 feet above sea level, between the Monadhliath Mountains and the Cairngorms, the town always offers a feeling of exhilaration. The towering summit of Creagh Dubh to the west is 2600 feet high and offers an excellent viewpoint. About a mile south of Kingussie are the ruins of Ruthven Barracks. Perhaps the main attraction in Kingussie is Am Fasgadh (Gaelic: the shelter), which is the Highland Folk Museum, now undergoing much-needed renovations and new presentation methods for the many exhibits of Highland life collected over the years.

The museum is housed in the 'Old Lodge', a white-harled Victorian residence, and a number of modern annexes made necessary as the result of recent acquisitions. The idea of the museum was developed by Dr I. F. Grant, Edinburgh, who, after seeing the methods used by the peoples of Scandinavia to preserve their living past, decided to organize a similar institution for the Highlands of Scotland. She had a disheartening start in a disused church on the island of Iona, off the coast of Mull, and her growing collection of exhibits was eventually moved to Laggan. By 1944 the exhibition was opened to the public in its present premises. The replicas of some of the old dwelling houses in the grounds of the museum are interesting. To ensure exactitude, one of the full-scale houses on view, a Lewis 'black house', was erected under the supervision of an old man who made the journey from Lewis for the purpose. It is a squat dwelling, ideally suited, with its design evolved over the centuries, for existing in the environment which obtains in Lewis. A rather more recent mason-built 'but and ben', of a type once common on the Scottish mainland, has also been erected in the museum grounds.

In the museum itself there are many items of interest for the naturalist, the sportsman and the social historian. One wing of the house contains examples of locally-produced textiles and linens. Primitive looms, spinning wheels, wool combs, spindles, cords and implements for scutching flax are shown. There is a display of plant dyes used in the colouring of thread for tartan and other cloths. A large part of the museum contains domestic articles which display the harmony with which man in the Highlands lived with natural things. Brooms and brushes are made from heather twigs, rushes, bent-grass and moss. Ropes were woven from horsehair, rushes and heather fronds as well as the roots of trees and shrubs. There are many beautiful examples of home-made wooden vessels made from birch and fir. The sides of cupboards, cabinets and chairs are constructed from oven oak scrub. Bent-grass appears in the form of pleated saddle-pads, chair seats and horse collars. There is a complete set of a pearl-fisher's implements including the clap-stick and flat-bottomed flask which tinkers used when searching the bed of the River Spey for its pearls. The great dependence of the old Highland population on the wild life of the countryside around them for the necessities of life is well demonstrated by this museum, which holds the key to the way of life and culture of the Gael. Behind the 'black house' in the grounds is a small 'clack' mill and a collection of dairying equipment. Crofting and farming implements and vehicles are displayed in a large new building, being the donation of the MacRoberts Douneside Trust.

Before the advent of the railway, Kingussie was the centre of a spinning and weaving industry, supported by the Duke of Gordon; but the venture failed. Fortunately, the Highland Railway terminus proved to be something of the nature of a salvation, for tourists discovered the town as a good centre for coach drives and walks in the Cairngorms, and Kingussie flourished. Ancient history abounds here, taking in the old Church of Kingussie, chapels and a monastery and, older still, stone circles and cairns. Of more recent vintage is the small industrial estate which produces goods ranging from craft items to precision engineering, providing much needed work in an area too dependent on tourism for its economic base.

Much of the life in Kingussie revolves round the excellent High School, an institution with an old history dating to before 1642 and still participating in education on a broad basis of interpretation of life in a place where the landscape dominates all. About the year A.D.1200, Kingussie (the name is derived from Gaelic meaning 'head of the pine forest') was created a parish. In 1451 King James II granted charters to erect crofts, with the centre of life being the old village of Ruthven. After the Forty-five, Ruthven began to decline in importance and Kingussie, the satellite village took on the dominant role. When the railway opened in 1880, Kingussie became the centre for the shooting season and the building of large houses was the order of the day. It is reckoned that between 1880 and 1900, some £200,000 of private capital alone was invested in building holiday villas.

Between Kingussie and Kincraig is the Highland Wildlife Park, where wild animals, with some connections with the old indigenous fauna of Scotland, roam about freely in some 260 acres. The animals on show include red deer, bison, Soay sheep, Highland cattle, Alpine ibex and roe deer. The Park was set up in 1972 with the object of building up a collection of Scotland's animals and showing them in a way which will promote an understanding of the important part they have played, or are playing, in the Highland life and landscape. The venture, which involved the investment of £125,000, was assisted by the Highlands & Islands Development Board, and is now established as one of the most important attractions in the Spey valley.

Almost something of an appendage, the tiny village of Pitmain was once renowned as a coach staging post: "The Inn of Pitmain is on one of the richest and most extensive farms, and is therefore plentifully supplied with every article desirable to travellers, and is fitted up with the best accommodations; and being in a situation of singular importance to Highland journeys, it is much frequented in the summer season." The old hostelry has now quite disappeared and Pitmain suffered as a direct result of the rise in the importance of Kingussie. It was also at one time an important gathering point for cattle before their long journey south to the cattle trysts at Crieff and Falkirk.

On the road to the west of Kincraig is Lochan Geal, the White Loch, which was at one time famed for its huge pike; tradition also has it that there were to be caught in it trout covered with hair. These seemingly legendary fish were thought to be a figment of the popular imagination. However, fish have been caught which were found to have tiny hairs on their scale tips. In certain conditions of light, the fish can look as if they are indeed hairy. Kincraig is now deeply involved in the tourist trade, as it was nearly a century ago, though now the tourists tend to be nomadic rather than semi-residential. A note by an observer last century says: "Perhaps few places in Scotland can boast of such lovely birches as are to be seen about Kinrara and Aviemore, or near the mouth of the River Feshie". Kincraig was originally called Boat of Insh, where one obtained a ferry to cross the Spey at the north end of Loch

Insh. But the building of a bridge made the ferry redundant. The Spey was crossed at Boat of Insh by Queen Victoria in September 1860. Loch Insh, nearby, was at one time the home of very large pike and the loch was regularly netted. There is a mention of some sixty salmon being taken in at one haul — halcyon days compared to the present when salmon are so scarce due to factory fishing and netting in the free-for-all oceanic waters outside territorial limits.

The Loch Insh marshes are now a nature reserve. The acres of overspill water provide an ideal environment for wild swans, whose dramatic calls herald the arrival of winter on Speyside. The marshes are an important wintering place for wild Whooper swans. This 1200-acre reserve, half of which is owned by the Royal Society for the Protection of Birds and half leased from local owners, provides a sanctuary for nearly ten percent of all Whooper swans which come to Britain in winter. The largest of our migratory water fowl, they breed in Iceland and arrive in Speyside in early October, having made the long haul over dangerous waters of the North Atlantic in one gruelling flight. This feat is quite incredible, not only as a physical effort, but especially as a navigational achievement, when it is remembered that many of the migrants are young birds which have had the practice of flying only a few miles before they embark on their trans-ocean journey. The swans stay until late April or early May. The reserve is closed to visitors during the winter, though the birds can be seen easily from a number of vantage points on the main roads on both sides of the marshes.

Tor Alvie, on the east side of the A9 from Loch Alvie, is a wooded hill on the summit of which is the Waterloo Monument, erected to commemorate Colonel Sir Robert MacAra of the 42nd and Colonel John Cameron, of the 93rd Highlanders and their brave countrymen who fell at Waterloo. The Tor also supports the weight of a monument each to a former Duke and Duchess of Gordon. The hill has another claim to fame: it was climbed by Prince Leopold, afterwards King of the Belgians, when on a visit in 1819.

A place now milling with tourists, Aviemore has been wrenched into modern times by the building of the Aviemore Centre. About 150 years ago, the inn at Aviemore was described thus: "There was no such inn upon the road; fully furnished, neatly kept, excellent cooking, the most attentive of landlords, all combined to raise the fame of Aviemore. Travellers pushed on from the one side, stopped short at the other, to sleep in this comfortable inn." But with the opening of the Highland Railway between Perth and Forres, the inn fell into disuse and was closed. However, the geographical situation of Aviemore was to be an asset in its favour, and the later opening of the direct line to Inverness via Carrbridge made Aviemore an important railway junction which was recognized in the new houses that were soon built to accommodate visitors. Its situation was always extolled:

> As one steps from the train at Aviemore after a long night journey from the South, one's travel-tiredness is instantly dispelled by the wonderful air of Upper Speyside. It blows across to the Strath direct from the High Cairngorms that stand mist-swept or clear, according to the weather, a few miles to the south. Spring and Summer often come together in this Highland glen. One week the birches are leafless as at mid-Winter, then comes a succession of warm sunny days when the hill burns of the Cairngorms are full to the brim with snow water and the air is balmy even to the hill tops. The birches instantly respond to the summer spell, and the trees clothe themselves with filmy green and drench the air with their perfume. After a shower at the end of an early June day the scent of the Aviemore birches is one of the most exquisite things in nature. But as the trees grow to their full foliage the perfume lessens and after mid-Summer it hangs in the air only to a lesser degree.
>
> The glory of the broom is in June, and the rowans also are laden with scented bloom. In May and June there is no darkness in Strathspey. For an hour either side of midnight a soft twilight broods over the valley, but the Cairngorms are always visible, and the whole night echoes to the call of sandpipers, oyster catchers and green plover. For the hills there is no season like the early months of midsummer. The high tops have still much snow about them, and the alpine plants are commencing to flower.

Despite the massive development of tourist facilities in the area, the landscape is still able to provide that kind of atmosphere, and, despite the scarring which has occurred in some places, there is still the chance for those seeking solace to find it without going too far off the beaten track. The landscape in fact still dominates the visitation of over one million people a year to the area around Aviemore.

Before the last war, most of the tourists tended to be those of affluent means, joined by hill-walkers and rock-climbers, whose pockets were not so well lined and who haunted hill bothies and the youth hostel at Aviemore. Then came the war and its inevitable changes to mark the end of one tourist era and the beginning of an astonishing period marked, perhaps, by the Aviemore Station Hotel being burnt down in the late fifties. It began in a small way with an investigation into the possibilities of winter sports on the Cairngorms. A group of hoteliers got together to plan for an extension of the short summer season. Along with the Cairngorm Sports Development Ltd (which built the White Lady chairlift in 1963, and the newer Coire na Ciste chairlift), the local initiative transformed the winter scene in the Spey valley. Before long, hotels were finding themselves open all the year round. This change was not left unnoticed by the Scottish Development Department, in St Andrew's House in Edinburgh, and big commercial interests, mainly because so much had been achieved with local initiative and little outside financial assistance. What could be achieved, therefore, with a massive injection of capital? This interest was welcomed with caution, however, for there were fears among the local conservationist landowners that a mushroom growth would be harmful in the long run to the area.

One of the main initiators of speculative interests in the Spey valley was the late Lord Fraser of Allander. He had a habit of referring to natural scenery and wildlife assets as "the merchandise", an attitude of mind which tended to confirm fears that profit would be pushed far ahead of other considerations. However, powerful interests were involved. Political circles saw that a holiday complex based on Aviemore would satisfy three commercial and altruistic aims: to create a tourist magnet; to boost Scotland's tourist industry by building a centre that would attract overseas as well as home visitors; and to encourage economic development of this part of the Highlands by creating jobs and commercial opportunities that would stop the steady drift of population to the south. So politics combined with commerce to create the holiday complex at a cost of £2½ million, though the final cost was reckoned to be in the region of £5m. There was a hint, however, of unholy haste. Insufficient research had been carried out at the planning stage to find out just how big a development the Spey valley could absorb. Planners were accused by conservationists of putting the cart before the horse by attracting tourists into the area, creating problems with short-term solutions, without first arranging to channel them. In brief, the planners had introduced an element of urban planning, the only expertise they had, instead of planning for the countryside as a whole. The planning authority involved, the former Inverness-shire County Council, and the Scottish Development Department, failed to insist on the arrangements, constraints, the facilities and the amenities being provided. Rather they allowed uncontrolled tourist pressures to occur before anyone had thought really hard on how to deal with them.

But the project went ahead, to be built on a 75-acre site below the line of the Monadhliath Mountains: a complex of hotels, roads, chalet accommodation, caravan site, theatre-cum-cinema, ice-rink, shops, restaurant and other facilities, which together formed a self-contained new community in the middle of the existing and older-established Aviemore village community.

The feasibility of the Aviemore Centre, some ten years after its inauguration, is still a matter of debate. A private investment of some £3½ million was, by 1965, still unable to offer the investors a reasonable return on the capital outlay. What had been done, however, was to treble the local population figure, contributed well over £250,000 of spending power to the area, boosted the area's tourist industry with a strong international appeal, and provided many facilities which were lacking before the development. Further investment by the Highlands & Islands Development Board helped to diffuse the industry, centred as it was on Aviemore, to take in the whole of the Spey valley from Grantown-on-Spey to Dalwhinnie and Laggan. In a wider context, the Badenoch district which, as a whole, had been losing its population up until 1961, had an increase of 3000 in the decade following the opening of the Aviemore Centre in 1966, and this figure is still climbing. Much of the increase is due to the influx of newcomers as well as to local people from nearby areas who find work in the industry. The Centre itself now employs about 600 people, a not insignificant figure, though it is often difficult to find local people in the middle and higher echelons of management grades.

One problem which has been created because of the sheer size and complexity of the centre is that relating to the effect it has had on small hotels and enterprises. One hotelier, who was in at the beginning of the development of the ski facilities, now finds himself having to push harder for custom. Specialist shops in the centre tend to attract more custom than is healthy for similar small retail outlets outside the centre. It is often difficult to get good quality staff and to compete with the wages offered at the centre. One further objection to the development, as viewed from a stance of 'ten years on' is the impact on the communities in the Spey valley, where the dominant emphasis on tourism has become something of a Gulliver in the land of Lilliput, and these communities have found their characteristics somewhat changed from the old days.

On the other side of the coin, there is doubt that the centre's national and international advertising has created a great deal of spin-off business for local enterprises. In other areas, too, there has been an impact. Before the centre opened, Aviemore Police Station consisted of a sergeant and two constables. Now it is manned round-the-clock by a staff of sixteen, including three sergeants. The milling tourist population inevitably brings crime in its wake; however, apart from a particularly nasty murder in 1976, crime is of the petty variety, mainly perpetrated by youngsters who tend to use the centre as a base for their forays. A target for the drug market, these young people have been caught up in this traffic, but as yet the problem has kept a low profile, and is being monitored by police.

When the Highlands & Islands Development Board introduced capital into the development of the Spey valley, there was a stated intention to initiate a study of the effect of the tourist impact on both people and landscape. After a complete silence for some years, early in 1978 it was announced that a comprehensive study of the impact of tourism in upper Strathspey was to be carried out by the Development Board and the Scottish Tourist Board. Some might say that it is rather late in the day to conduct such a study, but at least some long-term effects and trends can be analysed over the three years it is proposed to carry out the necessary research. The study will assess how successful tourism has been in creating jobs and income in the area, and whether the build-up in population and infrastructure resulting from the major tourism investment has made it possible to generate other forms of economic development. The study will also be concerned with the implications of tourism development for population structure and local community life. The study may well come to the conclusion that though material benefits have undoubtedly been accrued in the Spey valley, some important tangibles have been lost in the process of attracting a spending power of some £15 million annually into the area.

Although not strictly a village of the River Spey, Carrbridge does rest on the banks of the brawling River Dulnain, whose waters from the Monadhliath Mountains make no small contribution to the flood of the Spey. It is now an attractive village and was the pioneering focus of inclusive ski-ing holidays. In past decades the village was a thriving health resort, which boosted its trade when the Carrbridge section of the Highland Line was begun in 1890 and opened in 1892, though not before some trouble had been encountered and solved by the railway engineers. The line's approach to Carrbridge is through Crannich Wood where, close to the station, a massive area of peat moss was discovered. The weight of the railway embankment squeezed up the moss on both sides and it was not until some 50,000 cubic yards of extra solid material had been deposited in the pit was a good foundation for the rails secured.

Carrbridge was once an important staging post for the Inverness mail coaches travelling south across the northern, bleak and windswept spur of the Monadhliath Mountains. The site of the old inn is now occupied by a hotel. The River Dulnain is crossed at one point by an old arch, the origin of which was shrouded in mystery, though its roots were more firmly embedded in living rock on both sides of the river. It was in fact built c. 1776 by the Earl of Seafield for the purpose of carrying funeral parties over the Dulnain to the old churchyard at Duthil, after an incident when two local men were lost trying to cross the river in flood. Popular belief attributed the bridge to the Romans, though its architecture obviously indicated a much later period. General Wade, too, was given the credit for its construction; his bridge, in fact, is some two miles downstream.

The economy of Carrbridge is at present solidly laid on the rock of tourism; during the summer months the place is a veritable multilingual crossroads. On the south side of the village is the Landmark Visitor Centre, which attracts some 300,000 visitors each year. This is an American-style audio-visual exhibition which traces the natural history of the Highlands in a dramatic way. Visitors can walk through time via a series of darkened corridors where exhibits of Highland life in the past bring history vividly to the eye and ear. The centre was opened in June 1970, only to be partially destroyed by fire in May 1973. But a massive rescue operation was mounted and the new rebuilt centre was open again for business two months later. The centre has a nature trail on its doorstep, and caters for open-air picnics.

The name of Boat of Garten has long lost its visible origin:

the chain-operated ferry across the River Spey replaced by a bridge in 1899. But it retains its rural setting as a settlement which owes its existence to the opening of the railway in 1863. To the east is Loch Garten, now a reserve of the fish-eating osprey. Although the village is a youngster in the Spey valley, dating from the 1860s, there is close by the site of medieval fortifications known as Tompitlac, the name containing the tell-tale element 'pit', indicating a site of Pictish origin. There is little of the original structure to be seen now, save a moat which can just be traced.

The village is now the base for the Strathspey Railway, yet another enterprise which is tapping the tourist potential of the Spey valley. The rail link between Aviemore, Boat of Garten and Forres was opened in August 1863; the section connecting Boat of Garten and Forres closed in October 1965, to be lost but not forgotten. The idea of re-opening the Aviemore – Boat of Garten section was mooted by the Highlands & Islands Development Board, as part of its scheme of things to diversify tourist facilities in the Spey valley. In 1967 the Scottish Railway Preservation Society was invited to participate in the re-opening plans and, after a period of negotiation with British Railways, it made an offer for the line; but this fell through, to be rescued in 1971 by a group of railway enthusiasts who formed the Strathspey Railway Company in that year. A year later an agreement was reached to purchase the line for £44,000, with the Development Board putting up a grant of £10,000 and a loan of £20,000. The total coast of re-opening the line, including the purchase of the line, stock and other equipment, will probably reach some £80,000.

As the company members found out, to re-open a railway line in Britain these days is fraught with problems, not the least of which is the preparation of a Light Railway Order which has to be granted by the Department of the Environment before passengers can be carried in the rolling stock. Restoration work on the line began in 1972, together with the refurbishing of Boat of Garten station to its former glory, which had lain dilapidated and derelict for eight years. All the work was carried out voluntarily by the company's members and other helpers, about 400 in all, who have restored some twelve steam and seven diesel locomotives and about fifteen coaches. In addition to attending to the task of laying new rails, renewing sleepers, renovating signals and doing up the station, the Strathspey Railway Company has been collecting items of railway interest. The intention is to make Boat of Garten station a railway museum. This is more than appropriate because the village was built for the railway and its original tenants were railway officials and workers. A rent receipt for one house issued by the Great North of Scotland Railway, dated in the 1880s, was found recently in Boat of Garten, and is now part of the museum exhibits.

But while history forms the background to the company's activities, the present and the future are of equal concern, mainly because the company requires sources of revenue to maintain their operation. To this end, the company are to run the section of line between Aviemore and Boat of Garten as a commercial operation, carrying fare-paying passengers in coaches pulled by steam engines and offering at Boat of Garten a time-slip into the past. It is this kind of effort which has proved so successful in other parts of the country, and where the efforts of British Rail have failed so miserably, perhaps, because a purely commercial stance has been taken without recognizing that history can make a profit if it is well organized, presented and interpreted sympathetically. As it is, the Strathspey Railway Company and the Strathspey Railway Association, whose members have played a vital part in the restoration of the line, have fulfilled an important role and have given the visitor to the Spey valley an interesting visual contact with the past.

In sharp contrast to Boat of Garten, a mere upstart of last century, Nethy Bridge has a history of settlement going back many centuries, which includes the era of the Lairds of Grant with their 'tails' of Highlanders, who dispensed justice of the roughest kind through baron bailies who tried local transgressors and administered the law, as they saw it, in a freestyle interpretation. Standing on the banks of the Nethy, the village, with Coulnakyle, a much smaller settlement, had a close association with the operations of the York Buildings Company (*see* Chapter VI). The company had an iron-ore smelting furnace on the banks of the Nethy, the ore for which was carried all the way from the Lecht, beyond Tomintoul. At the turn of this century, nearly two hundred years after the company had collapsed in 1735, the 'Iron Mill Croft' still displayed the solid remains of the beams and framework of the original structure, though much had fallen into the river bed by that time. The site can still be seen, however.

Near the village, a mile or so along the Grantown road, is Abernethy Church, dedicated to St George with a prized possession in the form of an old stone font of uncertain age. Documentary evidence of the original settlement of Nethy Bridge dates from 1461 in a document containing the name 'Abirneithi', which was a focal point for commercial and economic activities at that time. The present village grew up on the site of much older buildings; an indication of this newer growth being the original name of the village as Bridge End.

Just north of an almost semi-circular bend in the River Spey is Grantown-on-Spey, which owes its origin to the efforts of the Laird of Grant in establishing a new economic focal point for the fertile area in which the town stands at present. The first public notice of the Laird's intention appeared in the *Aberdeen Journal* on Monday 15th April 1765:

Sir Ludovic Grant and Mr Grant of Grant propose a TOWN should be erected and will give feus of long Leases, and all proper Encouragement to Manufacturers, Tradesmen, or others, sufficiently recommended and attested as to Character and Ability, who incline to settle there. – The Place proposed for the Town is called Feavoit, to which the Fair and Markets in the neighbourhood can be collected. It will be the more convenient, as it lies near to Spey Bridge, has Public Roads branching off from it to Inverness, Nairn, Forres, Elgin, Keith, Braemar, Perth, and to the West Highlands, being eighteen Miles from Inverness, and twelve Miles distant from Forres.

Those who incline to settle, on Enquiry will find that it is a good, pleasant country, and well accommodated with all materials for building, lies near plenty of Moss and other Firing, has the Woods of Abernethie and Glenchernick near it, and a fine Limestone Quarry easily wrought. It is particularly well situated for all Manufacturers of Wool or Linen, being a great sheep Country; the Linen Manufactory already introduced, the soil good, and having fine Water and every conveniency for Bleach-fields. The situation is also well adapted for Wood Merchants, Carpenters, Cart Wrights, etc, the Woods lying near, and to be had at low Prices, and at a very moderate Charge floated down Spey to Garmouth, where Shipping may be easily had. Beside what is to be feued or let in long Leases those settling at the above Place may have, in Tack, cultivated or improveable Grounds, for their further Accommodation. . . .

The new town was to be built on the site of an older settlement. Old Grantown, known as Castletown of Freuchie, was in existence before 1553 and stood about a half-mile south-west of Castle Grant, the ancient seat of the chiefs of Clan Grant. In 1694 King William III and Queen Mary ordained "the town formerly called Casteltown of Frequhie, now and in all time to come to be called the Town and Burgh of Grant, and to be the principal burgh of regality, a market cross to be erected therein, and proclamations to be made thereat".

However, this settlement never got off the ground and failed, to be revived again in the 1760s. The new venture succeeded, perhaps because of a different set of circumstances. In 1766 the new town was planned on a grid system of streets " . . . planned out and marked off ground in lots or tenements for a village upon a barren heath moor, about an English mile or a little more south-west from the house of Castle Grant, and said year some of these lots or tenements were taken and houses erected". By the 1780s, Grantown, under the watchful eye of the "good Sir James" had become a prosperous centre of the Highland linen industry and had, in addition, become the main market town for a large part of the Spey valley. As well as linen, woollen cloths were produced, some of which gained an export market as far afield as West Africa. Towards the end of the century the linen industry here failed, as it did elsewhere, in the competing face of cheap cotton from the Americas. But sufficient impetus for growth had been established and the town went on to expand to become one of the finest planned towns in the north of Scotland. Indeed, by the middle of last century it had grown to such an extent that it rivalled Inverness, to become the second largest town in the county. Further impetus was given to Grantown by the visit of Queen Victoria in 1860 (she paid "an amusing and never to be forgotten visit"). In 1863 the railway arrived to set the seal on the town's reputation as a base for visitors.

As with all the schemes of men, the original inducements held forth by the promoters were more of a promising than a permanent nature. Indeed, had a similar advertisement appeared in the pages of our modern newspapers, the promoters might well have found themselves in court for gilding the lily; for example, "shipping" was not "easily had" at Garmouth, and the "materials for building" were not up to the correct standards. Even so, the present population of some 1600 inhabitants will agree that the town has gained more than it has lost in its two centuries of existence.

The town is a planning delight, particularly the Square, which is a town centre almost without equal in the Highlands. The trees are nearly one hundred years old, and are beautifully belying their age. The Square, the former market-place, was given to the townspeople to mark the bicentenary of the founding of Grantown. Some of the oldest buildings in the town line the Square. At the north-west corner is an eighteenth-century house with double windows, a reminder of the days when house-owners were imposed with a window-tax. The granite-built Speyside House, built to replace a former eighteenth-century orphanage, has clean sharp lines which more than please the eye. The clock under the cupola was paid for out of funds collected for soldiers in the Napoleonic Wars; but by the time the fund had reached its target, hostilities had ended, and the clock was installed as an *aide-mémoire* for the townspeople.

With the increase in the tourist industry, it was inevitable that Grantown would look for its fair share of business, and this it has managed to obtain, despite the fact that it is off the main A9 route to Inverness. Most of the usual 'offices' for tourists are offered. Recent incomers to Grantown have brought new craft skills with them, and now glass-blowing, pottery and other crafts are offered to the tourist traffic. Part of the R.A.F. School of Physical Training is based in Grantown to give survival courses for air crews, with training in map and compass work. The nearby Cairngorms are an ideal testing ground for these men. A rather nice public relations touch is the annual tidying-up campaign organized by the School; parties make for the Cairngorms and clear up litter left after the main tourist season has ended. About 1000 volunteers each year go through a number of days of hard physical torture in courses aimed at building character, resilience, leadership, physical fitness and an ability to mix with others in a situation of mutual hardship. The School caters for both sexes, with the women taking part in exactly the same outdoor activities as the men. Volunteers are carefully selected for the course, which means that very few fail to emerge successful from the tests of stamina. A typical week's activities could include two days' trekking over the Cairngorm peaks (18 miles a day) with a 40-lb pack on the back; a day's canoeing on the Spey (8 miles); a day's mountaineering and a day's orienteering. Mornings can begin with a five-mile run at 06.30 hours. The School is run by the R.A.F. Physical Education Branch and recently there have been visits by members of the French Air Force.

While shinty is 'the game' south in Badenoch, curling is the sport in the Grantown area. This ancient game was inaugurated in the Valley of Strathspey in 1856 and in the following year the Strathspey Club was affiliated with the Royal Caledonian Club, since when curling has been the main winter sport in the area, now somewhat ousted by ski-ing, but still not lacking in its many adherents and enthusiasts. It is said that more outdoor curling is enjoyed by the Grantown-on-Spey Curling Club than any other club in Scotland. The main Curling Bonspiels of the North of Scotland are held each year at Grantown, when as many as 400 players are on the ice for the day's playing.

From Spey Bridge, the Spey wanders like a serpent in its northerly course, overlooked on the eastward side by the Hills of Cromdale, or Haughs, celebrated in Scotland's history and folksong. In 1690 the Highlanders who had risen up in support of King James II and who had annihilated the English at the Battle of Killiecrankie in 1689, were themselves defeated by troops under the command of Sir Thomas Livingstone, fighting for King William:

> As I cam in by Auchindoun,
> A little wee bit frae the town,
> When tae the Highlands I was boun',
> To view the Haughs o Cromdale.

> I met a man in tartan trews,
> I spier'd at him what was the news;
> Quoth he, "The Highland army rues
> That ere they cam to Cromdale".

So runs the folk song which is as popular today as it was almost three centuries ago; so crushing was the defeat that it remains fresh in folk memory. The Battle of Cromdale was fought on 1st May 1690. General Buchan had been despatched in the cause of King James to lay waste the Low Country of Scotland and arrived on 30th April at Lethendry, just south of Cromdale, where he encamped after placing guards near the old village church. Meantime, Sir Thomas Livingstone, who had been stationed at Inverness, arrived with his troops at Derraid, near Castle Grant, on 1st May by break of day. They crossed the Spey by a ford below Dalchapple, not unobserved by Buchan's guards at the church. Then the King's forces made the attack before the Highlanders could either dress themselves or prepare for action. It was scarcely a battle, more a rout. Some of the Highland fugitives took refuge in Lethendry

Castle, near the battlefield, and were there made prisoners. Others were overtaken at Aviemore; while another detachment were prevented in laying siege to Loch an Eilean Castle.

The Haughs are a northern rock peninsula of the Cairngorm range and separate the River Spey from its tributary, the Avon. The small village of Cromdale belies its claim to history. It was originally a settlement with a church as its nucleus and was known as Kirktown of Cromdale. Its importance was also due to the fact that it was a crossing place by ferry over the Spey. This accounts for the rather puzzling names in the area, of Nether Port, Upper Port, Upper Port, East Port, and West Port, all associated with the access routes to the river bank. In 1609 Cromdale was erected into "ane free burgh and baronie" by King James VI. It had its own courthouse, prison and a hanging hill (Tom na Croiche). The decay of Cromdale as a burgh is said to have been hastened by a market-day fight between rival factions of the Grants; after this incident, the Laird of Grant decided to build Grantown-on-Spey.

At Bridge of Avon, the River Avon joins the Spey, a convergence overlooked by Ballindalloch Castle, said to have been in its day one of the finest specimens of the Scottish baronial style. The oldest part dates from 1546; the building was completely restored in 1850. The grounds are famous for their displays of daffodils in the spring. When the castle was first built, its masons had a sore time of it. No sooner had the walls reached a certain height, when they were knocked down by some mysterious agency. So often did this happen that the Laird set up a watch during the night and found that in the early morning a great wind came down from nearby Ben Rinnes which not only whirled the half-built castle walls into the Avon, but pitched the Laird himself and his attendant into a holly bush. A demoniacal voice was heard to say, three times: "Build on the cow haugh". The Laird, mindful of what might happen if he ignored the order, then caused his new castle to be built on the low ground, instead of on the higher ground as he had wished.

The village of Charlestown of Aberlour was founded in 1812

by Charles Grant of Wester Elchies, on much the same lines as Grantown. Feus, with four acres of land attached, were granted on liberal terms and were soon in great demand. The channel of the Spey supplied some of the building materials needed for the houses, which certain rather frugal feuars carried to the new village in hand-barrows, with the assistance of their wives. The outstanding feature of this small burgh is the width of the main street, lined with trees. In older times the parish was called Skirdustan, from the old church there having been dedicated to St Drostan. The setting up of new settlements was a popular pastime in this area of the Spey valley, with Archiestown, Rothes, Fochabers, Tomintoul, Dallas, Cullen, Dufftown and Newmill, in Morayshire alone, all having similar origins. The Grant laird who set up Aberlour advised in 1760: "It is in the interest of every gentleman possessed of ane estate in the Highlands to collect a number of Mechanicks and other industrious people into some centricall spot". The advice was not lost on these estate lairds.

Aberlour thus began its late history with the "Mechanicks" or tradesmen congregating in the new town and setting up for business in its main street, which runs parallel to the Spey and which is also the main road from the lowlands of Moray to Grantown and Aviemore. The fall in population from 1200 or more in the 1930s and 1940s to about 800 today is due to a peculiar circumstance: the closure some years ago of the town's famous orphanage, which provided a home and upbringing for between 300 and 400 children drawn from many parts of Scotland.

Though much of the original local industry has now gone, Aberlour is in the heartland of the whisky country and boasts its own distillery. Indeed, from the hills to the east of the town, looking up and down the valley of the Spey, it is possible to see the smoke rising from a fair proportion of the 43 distilleries in the Moray District. Some would say that the best shortbread in the world is made in Aberlour, the product of a small bakery venture established in 1909. The shortbread is exported to several overseas countries, keeping a workforce of about 200 people busy. The shortbread is based on traditional recipes and made by traditional methods. The ingredients are simply flour, sugar, butter and salt, made into a magic mixture by decades of expertise.

Consolidating Aberlour's position as a focal community base is the Speyside High School, built at a cost of over £1½ million, so that children do not now have to travel long distances (at one time a 60 mile round trip to far-away Keith) for their education, and thus enabling the children to maintain their identities with the Spey valley.

North of Aberlour, at the junction of four main roads, is Craigellachie, with its splendid bridge which crosses the Spey in a rather elegant fashion. In the early years of last century, there was no bridge across the Spey between Fochabers and Grantown, some thirty miles inland. It was suggested by local landowners that Craigellachie would be the best site to rectify the lack and so Thomas Telford, bridge-builder *par excellence*, was asked to design something suitable. He came up with one of the most graceful bridges in the country. It was erected in 1815 at the modest cost (in present-day terms) of £8000. It is a prefabricated iron structure, whose parts were cast hundreds of miles away at Plas Kynaston in Wales, and then brought piece by piece to the Highlands. Telford took some good advice from the locals and built the bridge some five feet higher than he had originally intended. It was good advice because it was only by some inches that the bridge avoided being swept away in the Moray floods of 1829. For modern motor traffic, however, the bridge has always presented a problem, with its tight turn below a great cliff rising straight out of the Spey; it is soon to be made redundant by a crossing more suited to contemporary and future traffic needs.

From Craigellachie, the Spey winds its way northwards through low country to Rothes, passing through Arndilly, with Ben Aigan to the west. This eminence used to be part of Arndilly Estate, which was, for generations, noted for the magnificent and well-managed woodlands of fir, larch, spruce and oak, which successive owners had planted with an eye to the future. Arndilly House, glimpsed from the road, was built about 150 years ago by David McDowal Grant who, in his time, was one of the great 'improvers' in Banffshire, and who devoted a great deal of his time and money to the proper development and exploitation of his estates. Arndilly however, is much older. Under the name of Ardendol, it was the centre of its own parish as early as 1215, coming into the ownership of the Grants when it was bought by Thomas Grant, who had extensive properties in Banffshire. Grant was also the patron of a young unknown lad called James Fergussson, born in Rothiemay in 1715. From humble origins, the lad made progress with his education under Grant's watchful eye, to become the most famous astronomer in Scotland and to be respected as a scholar in such varied disciplines as politics, history, moral philosophy and mechanical engineering. Partly self-taught, he learned the rudiments of astronomy while looking after sheep on the hills. Grant seemed to attract unusual men about him. One was Alexander Cantley, Grant's butler, of whom Fergusson was to write: "He was the most extraordinary man that I was ever acquainted with, or perhaps shall ever see; for he was a complete master of arithmetic, a good mathematician, a master of music on every known instrument except the harp, understood Latin, French, and Greek let blood extremely well, and could even prescribe as a physician upon any urgent occasion." With all that to his credit, one wonders why Cantley found the harp so difficult to play.

The village of Rothes on the east bank of the Spey was founded in 1766, on the site of a hamlet of ancient origin close by the castle of Rothes. It was basically a crofting community with no aspirations to commercial greatness until, in 1840, when J. & J. Grant Ltd, built a distillery to produce the famous Glen Grant whisky. The old castle, now ruinous, was built about the thirteenth century and was inhabited until 1622. Originally the stronghold of the Barony of Rothes, it was occupied by the Polocs or Pollocks, who were then overtaken by a succession of aspirants to power until it fell into the hands of the Earls of Seafield. King Edward I spent some time at the castle in July 1296 on his way south after a punitive expedition in the north.

From Rothes, the Spey takes a turn to the north-east to reach Boat of Brig. The rather curious conjunction in this name of two methods of crossing water is due to the fact that an old bridge across the Spey at this spot fell into decay and was replaced by a ferry-boat, which came to be known as 'the boat of the bridge'. This old bridge is said to have been the first, and for many years the only, bridge that spanned the Spey. Records of its existence date from the thirteenth century.

Two important centres of population to the east of the Spey, and connected to it by tributaries, are Dufftown and Tomintoul. Dufftown, situated at the convergence of the River Fiddich and Dullan Water, was founded in 1817 by James Duff, fourth Earl of Fife, hence its name. He had, however, originally called the new settlement Balvenie, after the nearby thirteenth-century Balvenie Castle; but the present name came into popular use a few years later. The Castle of Balvenie is said to have belonged to, successively, the Comyns, the Douglasses and the Stewarts of Athole, and was an occasional residence of the Wolf of Badenoch. Almost from its beginning Dufftown was a centre of the whisky trade. Seven malt distilleries founded here before the end of the nineteenth century are still prospering today; one, Mortlach, is one of the oldest in Scotland, founded by George Gordon and James Findlater, who took out a licence in 1823, the year of the Act of Parliament which regularized the trade and helped to stamp out the distillation of illegal brews. To the south of the town in the rise of Meikle Conval (1867 feet), on whose summit, in the old smuggling days, the folk of Dufftown used to light fires to warn the distillers in Glen Rinnes that the excisemen had just passed through. Mortlach Church is built on the site of where, in the sixth century, a church and school were founded by St Moluag of Lismore. The church was still there in 1010 when Malcolm III of Scotland extended it "to three spearlengths" in gratitude for a victory achieved over the invading Danes in the valley of the Dullan Water. For some years until the early twelfth century, Mortlach was the seat of a bishop. The present building dates from before the Reformation, but was later renovated and enlarged at various times. One of its fine stained-glass windows is in the memory of Lord Stephen, a Dufftown lad who made his fortune in Canada. Born in 1829, he was apprenticed to a draper and then, after working in Aberdeen, Glasgow and London, he emigrated to Montreal where he eventually became President of the Bank of Montreal and later was to join his cousin, Lord Strathcona, in the financing of the Canadian Pacific Railway.

Tomintoul is set between the Avon and the Conglass Water in one of the loveliest glens in the Highlands. It came into existence through the efforts of Alexander, the fourth Duke of Gordon. Situated some 1160 feet above sea level, the bracing air has made it a popular holiday town. Created in 1776, it remained for long a 'primitive town', and earned for itself some cruel observations from both Queen Victoria and James Hogg, the Ettrick Shepherd, the latter describing Tomintoul in his *Tales and Sketches:*

> We came to a large and ugly-looking village called Tomintoul, inhabited by a set of the most outlandish ragamuffins that I ever in my life saw; the men were so ragged and rough in their appearance, that they looked rather like savages than creatures of a Christian country; and the women had no shame nor sense of modesty about them, and of this the Highland soldiers seemed quite sensible and treated them accordingly.

The village has come a long way since that time and is now established as a centre of economic activity based on tourism, whisky distilling, farming, forestry and limestone quarrying. Tomintoul has another claim to fame, for it is linked in the national mind with Cockbridge, its neighbour at the southern end of the infamous Lecht road. The worse the weather, the more mentions these two villages get, the road often being the first in Scotland to be rendered impassable at the first drop in temperature, to become snowed up for long periods at a time.

The year 1937 was particularly bad and is still remembered by the older folk of the village. The village was cut off for six weeks, with the snow on the road to Tomintoul level with the telephone wires and up to the tops of house doors. Hill ponies had to be used to get about for essential supplies. Today, in summer, there is little thought for the hardships of these severe winters, which still occur, and tourists enjoy the unique atmosphere provided by river, forest, hill and moor.

After leaving Boat of Brig, the Spey enters the last lap of its journey from Loch Spey, where mountains are replaced by low hills and the last major human settlement is reached: Fochabers, on the east bank, with Gordon Castle to its north. For centuries the whole of this district was part of the extensive estates of the Dukes of Gordon, which at one time extended all the way from the Moray Firth to Ben Nevis in Lochaber, interrupted only by a two-mile strip in Rothiemurchus which belonged to someone else. Their thousands of acres in Strathspey took in the great forest of Glenmore. Although the income from rents, salmon fishings, grouse moors and forestry concessions was considerable, in 1785, the fourth Duke of Gordon found himself in sore need of cash and he sold the standing timber in Glenmore Forest to William Osbourne from Hull for £70,000. The latter built a shipyard at Garmouth and set up a successful business with a partner.

The Gordons have a colourful page to themselves in Scotland's history. When Robert Burns visited Gordon Castle on his Highland Tour, he wrote:

> Wildly here without control,
> Nature reigns and rules the whole.

Later, someone was moved to write that these lines "would be a more accurate description of the private lives of the Gordons of that time, than of the parish itself".

The fourth Duke of Gordon and his Duchess were quite a pair. He occupied most of his time in raising regiments and companies for the British Army, while the Duchess busied herself in scheming and plotting to marry her daughters off to the richest noblemen in the country; she was not successful. Between them, the Gordon pair had a staggering amount of illegitimate children, apart from legally-begot offspring. Names were a problem, particularly with two sons named George, a problem solved by the Duchess referring to them as "the Duke's George" and "my George". It was the Duke's George who succeeded to the title, but he proved to be no better at managing his affairs than his father. When he died, the last of his line, in 1836, he owed the not inconsiderable sum of £45,000 to the Royal Bank of Scotland. His titles and estates went to the Duke of Richmond, who also took the name Gordon. When he died in 1935 the Gordon estate around Fochabers came into the possession of the Commissioners for Crown Lands, with the Forestry Commission taking over part of the estate for the Forest of Speymouth.

Gordon Castle is a sprawling affair, but is magnificent in an equally magnificent setting. The site was formerly known as the Bog of Gight. The castle, founded in 1498, was almost totally rebuilt by the fourth Duke of Gordon towards the end of the eighteenth century. The gardens were laid out as extensive and pleasant policies. Some holly trees were those of the original "Blue Bells of Scotland", with the "Highland Laddie" of the song being the Marquis of Huntly who accompanied Sir Richard Abercrombie to Holland in 1799 as Colonel of the 92nd Gordon Highlanders:

Oh, where, tell me where, is your Highland laddie gone?
He's gone with streaming banners, where noble deeds are done,
And my sad heart will tremble till he comes safely home.
Ah, where, tell me where, did your Highland laddie stay?
He dwelt beneath the holly trees, beside the rapid Spey,
And mony a blessing followed him the day he went away.

The town of Fochabers owes its origin to the removal of an older village by Alexander, fourth Duke of Gordon, to make way for the rebuilding of the old castle, in 1776. By the end of the century, the new village had taken shape and had got rid of its reputation of being 'a poor place', as Dr Samuel Johnson described it. Today it is a thriving community with much to underpin its economy, not least being the famous Christie's Nurseries and Baxter's Foods, the former dating from 1820 and the latter now a household word for good food products all over the world.

The passage across the Spey at Fochabers was known as Boat of Bog until 1804 when a handsome bridge of four arches was completed. The Spey flood of 1829 caused two of the arches to fall, due to gravel having been left under the piers when they were built. In 1823 the arches were replaced by a wooden span which did duty until 1854 when it was converted to an arch of cast iron. A new bridge was opened in 1972.

Garmouth, on the western bank of the Spey was erected into a burgh of Barony in 1587 by James VI. Montrose paid it two visits in 1645: in February of that year he plundered the village and in September he burned it. Though having little claim to fame in these modern times, in its day its history impinged on the larger canvas of Scottish events. Its palmy days were when the forests of Abernethy, Glenmore and Rothiemurchus were cut down by William Osbourne and the York Buildings Company. It then suffered a setback when the Spey decided to change the position of its outflow into the Moray Firth after the flood of 1829, a circumstance which brought Kingston-on-Spey into being as the port for Garmouth. Today it is a quiet attractive village, marred now by the occasional intrusive modern buildings.

Kingston owes its name to two Englishmen from Yorkshire who established the ship-building operations in the eighteenth century, one of whom came from Kingston-upon-Hull. Though small, it has its place in British history, for it was here that King Charles II landed to sign the historic Solemn League and Covenant, an act which he performed with great reluctance. For a long time Kingston comprised only the small dwellings of salmon fishers; then, as its importance increased, larger houses were built, rather foolishly, one might suppose, on the banks of the Spey. However, until 1829, the river had behaved itself and the mouth had remained stable for many years. But 1829 saw the great Spey floods which swept away many of Kingston's houses; some of the present-day buildings were erected with rubble from the ruins. One building in Kingston is old: Dunfermline House, known originally as Red Corff House, which dates back to the Middle Ages. The lower part of the building is believed to have been erected as a changing-house by the monks of Dunfermline Abbey, who manned the Priory of Urquhart. About 1780 an upper storey was added and it eventually became the headquarters of a flourishing shipyard business. A recent owner has restored the house to its former glory, a task that took some eighteen years.

The mouth of the Spey is a mass of shingle and sand bars produced by the sea drifting and moving beach material along the Moray Firth coastline. The shingle bar at Speymouth is particularly troublesome as it diverts the river rather close to Kingston; the houses on the bank are literally a stone's throw from the river. The bank is constantly being threatened by erosion and periodically cuts have to be made through the bar or spit to channel the river away from the village. One cut was made in 1962, with a further cut in 1974, thus keeping Kingston from slipping into the Spey.

It is perhaps characteristic of the Spey that even at its mouth it is determined to cause trouble, rather than be satisfied with a gentle and calm flow into the sea. After a tempestuous journey of nearly one hundred miles, one might think that the river's water would be exhausted and content to reach the anonymity of the Moray Firth; but rather it is determined to maintain its identity to the last, by imposing its capricious will on the settlements of mere humans.

# IV

## TRIBUTARY WATERS

WHILE the River Spey takes all the credit for its journey through Strathspey from the head waters of Loch Spey through the valley, its fame is in no small measure due to the waters which are contributed to its flow by other rivers. Some of these rivers are of considerable length and volume and most have an interesting history of their own, often, in some respects, more significant than that of the Spey. It would thus be an injustice if one were to ignore the significant contributions which these rivers have made. More often than not, these tributaries of the Spey find their head waters in glens high up in the Cairngorms for the most part, though the impetuous Dulnain derives its source from the western heights of the Monadhliath Mountains.

One of the most southerly tributaries is the River Truim, which begins with its headwaters in Drumochter and flows north-west to join the Spey at Newtonmore. Its birthplace is the Sow of Athole and the Boar of Badenoch, fitting names for a river which finds its way into the Spey valley. It rises on the Inverness-Perthshire boundary on An Torc, about 2500 feet above sea level. It takes a northward course of some fifteen miles to meet the Spey and its route runs almost parallel with the main road and rail links into the Highlands. The Truim itself is contributed to by the waters of Allt Cuiaich, a stream which has its chief source in Loch na Cuiach on the slopes of Meall na Cuaich (3120 feet), a prominent round-topped hill seen from many parts of Badenoch. Glen Truim itself tends to be rather monotonous and desolate, the scene being relieved

80

only when the land falls away and the lower hills present a more varied vegetation. The falls of Truim, just south of Etteridge, present an attractive sight though they give no end of trouble to the salmon which try to pass up the river in times of low water. The Crubenmore Bridge in Glen Truim has recently been the subject of some restoration work by voluntary groups. The bridge, some 200 years old, once carried the A9 roadway from Perth to Inverness and was superannuated in 1928 when a concrete structure carried the burden of the road. The attractive structure of two superb arches was noticed to be falling into decay some time ago and it was thought only a matter of time before the bridge would collapse. So voluntary organizations, spurred on by the Scottish Rights of Way Society, got together to save the bridge for posterity. Volunteers from the Polmont Conservation Corps began repairs by damming the river to allow them to build up the foundations of the bridge, in particular the upstream cutwater which had been eroded by river swell and frost damage. Then came the replacement of the parapets which had been thrown into the river by mindless vandals. The volunteers camped beside the bridge during the restoration work, some working eight hours a day for seven days a week – for the princely sum of 40p a day. Some help was made available by the contractors who were working on the realignment of the A9, which has made the 1928 structure redundant (perhaps to be made the subject of another conservation task 200 years hence, who knows?). The contractors provided earth-moving machinery and materials, as well as scaffolding, free to the volunteer repair force. What makes the project interesting is that the Polmont Conservation Corps is made up of boys and staff from Polmont Borstal Institution, the boys willingly making some contribution to the society that has organized itself in such a way that nonconformists find themselves taken into the society's care. The date of the Crubenmore Bridge is not certain. It has been suggested that it was constructed after the period when General Wade and his successors built their roads and bridges, which ended in 1780; and it does not seem young enough to be a parliamentarian bridge, built when Parliament took the responsibility for the highways in 1803. Now with the restoration, the Countryside Commission for Scotland is planning to transform the immediate area into a permanent picnic site.

Just south of the place where the Truim meets the Spey is Invernahavon, where a famous clan fight took place in 1386. The cause of this particular fracas was the refusal of the Camerons of Lochaber to pay rent to the Mackintoshes of Clan Chattan for certain lands which the former held in Lochaber. The Mackintoshes decided that if the money was not to be forthcoming, then they would take the rent in cattle. So they organized a raiding expedition to collect, somewhat forcibly, the rent due to them. The Camerons, not surprisingly, took umbrage at the method used and chased the Mackintoshes, with the Davidsons, another Badenoch clan, to Invernahavon. There the Mackintoshes appealed for help to the Macphersons, the other prominent member of the Clan Chattan Federation. The latter agreed but found themselves allotted an inferior place on the battlefield and they withdrew in a huff, to become spectators rather than participators. Eventually they were persuaded, being wooed by a Mackintosh bard who plied them with such poetic appeals that they rejoined the fight to rout the Camerons just when the latter were on the point of victory.

To the west of the Truim, a smaller stream, Mashie Water, ten miles long, rises on Meall Cruaidh (2941 feet), a hill on the west side of Loch Ericht. For the most part this river runs through wooded land before it joins the Spey a little west of Laggan Bridge. The waters of the Mashie are taken into a conduit of the North of Scotland Hydro-electric Board near Strath Mashie House, whence it is piped westwards to feed the River Pattack and then emptied into Loch Laggan. Strath Mashie is one of the shortest straths in the Highlands.

The River Tromie, about twenty miles long, rises on the borders of Perthshire. It has two principal head-streams, Amhainn Gharbh Ghaig and Allt na Craoibhe, which combine to form Loch an t-Seilich, from which issues the Tromie River. This is the district of Gaick, the scene of the strange

happening mentioned in chapter five which befell the Black
Captain John Macpherson of Ballachroan and his hunting
friends. Glen Tromie offers a breeding area for the scarce twite.
A footpath from Blair Atholl takes one through to Kingussie.
This is in fact an old route to the north and is the only road to
the north shown on Green's map of 1689 and Moll's map of
1725. It was superseded by the military road over the
Drumochter Pass constructed by Wade in 1728-30, although
after that date the Minigaif Pass still appeared on maps as a
"summer road to Ruthven", to reach the Ruthven Barracks.
The route is about twenty-eight miles from Kingussie to Blair
Atholl and presents some of the most interesting scenery in the
Highlands, to say nothing of an abundance of wild life. On the
east side of the glen is a hill named Croidh-la, across the face of
which is a large and unusual rock formation. This is best seen
from Kingussie on a clear day; though some five miles away, it
extends to about a half mile to the south and it presents
something of the shape of a horse, facing south. The Glen
Tromie pathway is often hindered by rock falls. In 1922 an
avalanche occurred near where the fated Black Captain's bothy
stood, at the south end of Loch an t-Seilich, which killed
several hinds. The loch here is noted for its large trout; salmon
reach here this far from the mouth of the Spey.

The River Feshie discharges its waters into the Spey just
north of Loch Insh and Kincraig after a journey of some
twenty-two miles, which begins on the borders of Perthshire,
on Leathad an Tobhain (2994 feet). This glen route connects
to Braemar via Glen Geldie, a distance of some thirty miles.
The Feshie is fed by dozens of mountain streams, some of
particular significance and with spectacular waterfalls. The glen
has many associations with history and personalities. It was at
one time among the most important deer forests in the
Highlands and as such it attracted the hunting fraternity last
century. Sir Edwin Landseer, the father of Speyside tourism,
haunted the locality around the confluence of the Feshie and
Allt Coire Bhlair to make the sketches which were later to
form the bases for his famous paintings. One of the waterfalls

on this river was the subject of one of Landseer's pictures and it is known as Landseer's Falls; it is over 130 feet high. The rise in this area, Sron na Ban-righ, is associated with a tradition which led to the burning of much of the old forest hereabouts. Queen Mary of Scots was hunting in the district and was offended by her husband, returning from a distant hunting expedition, asking about the state of the forests rather than enquiring as to his wife's welfare. At this slight she gave orders to set the forests on fire, and watched the conflagration from the summit of Sron na Ban-righ.

The Feshie's most important tributary is the River Eidart which has a fine waterfall near to its junction with the Feshie. It has been noted by geologists that the upper course of the River Feshie presents an excellent example of the shifting of a watershed and the capture of the head waters of a stream belonging to another river system. The Eidart, which joins the Feshie about a mile below where the latter river touches the boundary between Aberdeenshire and Inverness-shire, was once the head stream of that river; but the Feshie has gradually cut back its bed to the march between the two counties and captured the upper part of the River Geldie. Thus, the former head waters are now those of the Feshie, and the watershed between the basins of the Rivers Spey and Dee has been shifted more than six miles eastwards.

No less a personage than Queen Victoria passed through Glen Feshie – twice, in 1860 and in 1861. She wrote in her *Journal* (1860):

> The Feshie and the Geldie rise almost on a level, with very little distance between them. The Feshie is a fine rapid stream full of stones. As you approach the glen, which is very narrow, the scenery becomes very fine – particularly after fording the Etchart (Eidart), a very deep ford ... Then we came upon a most lovely spot – the scene of Landseer's glory – and where there is a little encampment of wooden and turf huts, built by the late Duchess of Bedford.... We were quite enchanted with the beauty of the view.

In 1861 she passed through the glen once more:

Brown waded through the Etchart leading my pony; and then two of the others, who were riding on another pony, dropped the whole bundle of cloaks into the water! ... I felt what a delightful little encampment it (the huts) must have been, and how enchanting to live in such a spot as this solitary wood in a glen surrounded by the high hills. We got off, and went into one of the huts to look at a fresco of stags of Landseer's over a chimney piece.

A road through Glen Feshie has always been an attractive if elusive proposition to those who feel that the Highlands should be 'opened up' more so than it is at present, to meet the requirements of the tourist industry. The conservationists, however, present their usual well-proportioned case against the proposal; they see the dangers to natural life in the opening up of new areas, fragile as they are, to the press of thousands of insentient boots. The Glen Feshie road was first proposed by General Wade in the first half of the eighteenth century, but he dropped it in favour of more logical routes to link north and south. In 1828, engineers Thomas Telford and Joseph Mitchell surveyed, for the Commissioners for Highland Roads and Bridges, the route through Glen Feshie as an alternative to the long detour through the Drumochter Pass to get from Perth to Inverness. But the high altitude of the watersheds and the ever-present danger from snow led to the plan being abandoned. The idea then lay dormant, with only an occasional mention in the Press, until after the Second World War. During this period the glen suffered from the customary disregard for things delicate and intrinsic in favour of the uncompromising needs of hostilities. Many of the old pines which had stood unharmed for centuries were felled by soldiers; lumber camps were set up, roads were driven up the hillsides and the salmon dynamited in the rivers. Towards the end of 1972 the proposal for a road through Glen Feshie to link Aberdeenshire and Inverness-shire was again aired. Officials on both sides of the glen thought the project feasible at a cost of £2½ millions, and that increased tourist traffic would produce the necessary incentive for central Government to come up with the cash. Certainly, such a road facility would offer a convenient link between the winter sports area in the Cairngorms at Glenshee and Beinn a' Bhuird. However, so far Glen Feshie remains inviolate and only time will tell whether yet another Highland glen, offering so much in its original state, will be breached by the eyes of motorists.

The River Druie empties its waters into the Spey at Aviemore. The head waters of this river are in the famous Cairngorm Pass of the Lairig Ghru. For the first part of its course it flows in places deep underground, presumably the result of the water burrowing into landslides of screes and earth which have occurred over the centuries. The two main tributaries of the Druie are the River Luineag, which drains Loch Morlich in Glenmore Forest Park, and Am Beannadh, which drains Loch Einich, 1650 feet above sea level, a deep mountain loch set in the arm-like fold of Sgoran Dubh Mor 2000 feet above the loch itself, Einich Cairn and Braeriach. Glen Einich was once settled in the summer with shielings, where the people lived while looking after their cattle grazing on the summer mountain pastures. A description of that inveterate sportsman, Colonel Thornton in 1804 tells us:

> The bothee or sheeling is a cottage made of turf; the dairy house where the Highland shepherds or graziers live with their herds and flocks .... Here they make butter and cheese and gather juniper berries. The whole furniture consists of a few horn spoons, their milking utensils, a couch formed of sods to lie on, and a rug to cover them. Their food oatcakes, butter or cheese, and often the coagulated blood of their cattle spread on their bannocks. Their drink milk, whey, and, sometimes by way of an indulgence, whisky.

On the summit of Creag Dubh, on the mountain ridge running between the glen and the Spey valley is Clach Mhic Calein, the Argyll Stone. The name traditionally dates from 1594 when the Earl of Argyll took an active part in the efforts of King James VI to quell the attempt of the Earl of Huntly to restore Catholicism as the recognized religion of Scotland. Argyll was commissioned to root out the Catholic perpetrators, but his forces were routed at the Battle of Alltacoileachan, in Glenlivet, in October 1594, and were compelled to retreat with all haste. On their way south, the defeated troops halted on the Sgoran Dubh ridge and, beside the tor, they rested and ate. From this vantage point they could see whether Huntly's troops were following them or not. But Huntly had decided not to give chase and Argyll's men were able to make their way home, but not before their stop on Creag Dubh was lodged in local tradition.

The source of the Druie is the pass known as the Lairig Ghru, one of the ancient right of ways in the Cairngorms from Speyside to Braemar; it is about twenty-eight miles long and it takes up to twelve hours of hard trekking to go from end to end, going along a well-trodden path marked by cairns on the higher reaches. These higher reaches of the pass are associated with visions of spectres, in particular the Brocken or Grey man of Ben Macdhui, who has been seen by too many people to be discarded as figments of an imagination intoxicated by the high mountain air. Many have experienced psychic impressions and some have actually heard the ghostly footsteps of the Fear Liath Mor, the Big Grey Man. Could it be that the very intimate and personal sense of loneliness, minute man amid the over-whelming peaks of the Cairngorms, generates in the human mind an intense desire for companionship, which then mani-fests itself in a spiritual paraclete to walk with them along the way through the rarefied air of the mountains? Mountaineers will tell you that this is the case; even the most hard-headed will confess to a feeling of exhilaration in such surroundings, where man has had no impact, and even his presence on the mountains is no more than a speck of dust in the aeons of time taken to form these ranges.

Loch Morlich, the source of the River Luineag, nestles among the trees of the Queens Forest in Glenmore Forest Park. There are no National Parks in Scotland as there are in England and Wales; but the Forest Parks in Scotland are ample compensation for the loss. This particular area has been developed for the use of the discerning tourist. The Queen's

Forest was so named in commemoration of the Silver Jubilee of King George V and Queen Mary in 1935. The land had been purchased twelve years previously by the Forestry Commission and the planting of the woodlands has been a continuous process since that date. Some 4000 acres grow trees ranging from one to forty years, along with the remnants of the old Caledonian Scots pine, which can be seen in groups or single trees of great age, up to 200 years. Perhaps the main problem here is that the forest attracts so many visitors who inevitably cause damage to the vegetation, a situation which can be seen on the shores of Loch Morlich. The problem is recognized, however, and attempts are being made to use new techniques to encourage the regeneration of vegetation to preserve some of the original conditions.

Glenmore was formerly a royal forest and latterly the hunting ground of the Stewarts of Kincardine. Now it is the home of the National Outdoor Training Centre which is sponsored by the Scottish Sports Council and provides courses intended to introduce, or further develop, skills in adults on a direct tuition basis in a number of outdoor pursuits which vary according to the season. The centre is one of the mountain rescue posts in the Highland region and the staff of the centre form the team. To the north of Loch Morlich is Reindeer House, the base of administration for the reindeer herd, with Mr Mikel Utsi as the chief overseer for the animals.

On the south-eastern side of Cairngorm lies Loch Avon, or A'an, the source of the River Avon, which is thirty-eight miles long and is the longest, as well as being the most important, tributary of the Spey, whose waters it enters at Ballindalloch. Loch Avon rests in a deep valley dating from the glacial period and is fed by streams of truly high birth: from Cairngorm, Ben Macdhui and Beinn Mheadoin. The river flows in an easterly direction until it takes a sharp turn northwards at Inchrory. Before the river enters Strathavon it passes the remote village of Tomintoul, established in 1750, and described by Queen Victoria in 1860 as " ... the most tumble-down, poor-looking place I ever saw – a long street with three inns, miserably

dirty-looking houses and people, and a sad look of wretched-
ness about it". Things have changed over the years and
Tomintoul, enjoying the bracing air at 1200 feet above sea
level, attracts many visitors who delight in the hospitality
found around here. The Livet Water joins the Avon, some of
its clear waters having been diverted to supply the many
whisky distilleries for which Glen Livet is justly famous. At one
time it was recorded that no fewer than 200 illicit stills were in
operation in this district, a situation which the excisemen had a
hard time to cope with, until the Glenlivet Distillery became
legal and operated to such a degree of success that it gave the
lead for others to follow the process of legitimization. After the
Reformation, the Braes of Glenlivet was the site of the only
Roman Catholic college in Scotland, based at Scanlan, on the
Crombie Water, a tributary of the Livet. It was a modest
turf-covered building and served its students well until 1726
when the students were dispersed by the military; but it was
re-opened the following year. Then came a period of harass-
ment. In 1746 the Duke of Cumberland sent a detachment of
soldiers to burn the place down, with the students fleeing to the
hills for safety. Another building was erected, to be
abandoned in 1799 for another site at Aquhorties which, in its
turn, gave place to Blairs College near Aberdeen.

But for a geological circumstance, the River Nethy might
claim Loch Avon as its source. Instead, it has at present to be
content with its origin on the Saddle of Cairngorm, much less
than a mile to the north side of Loch Avon. It has a run of
some fourteen miles to Nethy Bridge, through Strath Nethy
and the Abernethy Forest to enter the Spey a little above
Coulnakyle. This village has a continuous history going back
some 600 years. Edward I is said to have flaunted his banners at
the place; and the noisy troops of Claverhouse pitched their
tents here. Both General MacKay and Montrose made Coulnakyle their base. The old Chiefs of Grant lived here, and the
Baron Bailies, of the bad old days, held their courts here to
administer their rough justice. The managers of the old York
Buildings Company lived here, to look after the forest-felling

activities of the company and, later, to oversee the iron-smelting works built on the banks of the Nethy. Castle Roy, a ruin lying about a mile north of Nethy Bridge, is sometimes claimed as being one of the oldest castles in Scotland; it is believed to have been built by the Comyns or Cummings, and was occupied as late as the sixteenth century.

The River Fiddich, with its name closely associated with a brand of malt whisky, is the most northerly tributary of any importance on the eastern side of the Spey. It rises on the south-eastern slope of Corriehabbie Hill at an altitude of over 2300 feet, and lying at the head of Glen Fiddich. After a run of some eighteen miles it enters the Spey at Craigellachie. It passes by Dufftown, a distillery centre of some importance.

The River Dulnain is the only major tributary with a source on the west of the Spey, in the Monadhliath Mountains. It begins life on Beinn Breac, some 2200 feet above sea level, and immediately begins to collect the waters from a number of streams before it takes its name from Carn Dulnan, an eminence on its eastern bank. Its impetuous journey is through wild and hilly country, sparse and monotonous, until it reaches Inverlaidnan and Carrbridge, when it flows through flat land which has had to be embanked to reduce the effects of flooding. It enters the Spey at Dulnain Bridge. It is a particularly fast-flowing river, rising fast after heavy rain, and it is always peat-stained. At one time it was renowned for its salmon as indicated by an old account: "There comes no salmon in this water, but extraordinary much kipper, which are in abundance, that a gentleman thinks nothing to kill 160 in a night. They used to feast the Sheriff, and so escape the fine, but the Commonalty pay some little thing." The "kipper" here means salmon near or at the time of spawning.

The only other western tributary of the Spey, of minor importance, is the River Calder, which flows through Glen Banchor, the scene of some clearances last century.

# V

## WATERSHED OF HISTORY

As THEY do now, people have always found settlement in the valley of the Spey as a most attractive proposition; it comes as no surprise, therefore, to find traces of human habitation going back some 5000 years. After the Ice Age retreated, the first human traces found in the area are those of farming people, whose relics are traceable near Grantown and Cromar. Some centuries later, another group of settlers left visible evidence of their existence in standing stones and mounds, such as are found at intervals in Strathspey, at Raitts, Kincraig, Delfour, Ballinluig, beside Loch Alvie, Loch nan Carraigean, Loch Pityoulish, Street of Kincardine, Lynchurn, Congash near Grantown, Avielochan, Glenshee and Strathardle. In the few centuries B.C., Celtic settlers left a 'crannog' or artificial lake dwelling in Loch Kinord, and fortified structures also began to pepper the countryside, as can be seen at Avielochan and Laggan. Recorded history begins with the advance of the missionaries of the Celtic Church into the strath, to be followed by the period when the great families emerged: Shaws, Comyns, Grants, Mackintoshes and Macphersons, who also played significant roles in Scotland's national history. Then came the Fifteen and the Forty-five, bringing to the boil the succession of religious feuds and civil wars in Scotland, culminating in the shattering changes in the social structure of the Highland clans and the dark-edged Clearances, since when the strath emerged slowly into the light of a new age, for good and for ill, when communities no longer existed on their own, but were to become increasingly dependent on the outside for their

91

economic and social progress. Any visitor to Strathspey who
arrives with an open mind, ready to search and discover, will
find that the 'atmosphere' in the area is redolent with a taste of
the ancient past – despite the vast numbers of people thronging
the more popular parts of the valley, it is still possible, and easy
enough, to gain access to areas of loneliness where one can let
the imagination roll back a thick carpet of some five millennia
and marvel at the continuity of human settlement which has
shaped Speyside into what it is now.

One of the clearest ways in which the various peoples who
inhabited Strathspey in times past can be introduced is to look
at the evidence of place-names left on the map by early Celts,
Picts, Britons, Gaels and Normans. Place-names, because they
are first and foremost words, are first-order linguistic evidence
of the people who lived in a particular area. When the
Gaelic-speaking Scots began to arrive in Scotland from Ireland
from the fifth century A.D. onwards, they were not the first
Celts to settle here. Members of another branch of the Celtic
family of languages, the Picts, had already been in the country
for several centuries. The language of the Picts is said to be
fairly closely related to Gaulish, a Continental Celtic tongue.
In particular, the word *pett* (meaning part or share), where it
occurs, indicates the existence of Celtic-speaking Picts. While
the word occurs most frequently on the eastern seaboard of
Scotland, from the Firth of Forth to Aberdeenshire, it also
occurs in a few places in Strathspey (e.g., Pitmain and Loch
Pityoulish).

The intrusion of Gaelic speakers into the area is evidenced
by the occurrence of such name-elements as '*baile*' (village or
hamlet) and '*achadh*' (field), indicating those places where
settlement first took root. The element '*kil*' (cell or church)
tells us something of the movement of Irish Gaelic-speaking
missionaries, more than likely from Iona, among these early
peoples. '*Baile*' and '*achadh*' occur frequently in the northern
parts of the Spey valley, where the river runs through broad
meads and where the land was most fertile. The '*cil*' name
element is not so common, however, and where it is found it

is more in the southern reaches of the Spey, significantly close to the main access of Spey valley dwellers to the Great Glen and Lochness-side, where the name is very common.

North of the Forth-Clyde line, excluding modern Argyll, there are to be found monuments carrying designs on them which are so stereotyped that one cannot but fall to the conclusion that they carry symbolic meanings. These are the Pictish stones and their distribution tends to fit the old descriptions of the boundaries of the kingdom of the Picts as found described in Adamnan's *Life of Columba*, written in the late seventh century, and in Bede's *Ecclesiastical History*, written about a century later. It is now accepted as indisputable fact that these monuments(there are some 300 of them) were erected by the Picts and that the symbols refer to fundamental aspects of Pictish society and its structures and ceremonies. In the Spey valley the stones are to be found from the mid to the upper reaches of the Spey.

Two examples of the fortified places in the Spey valley occur at Laggan and at Avielochan. The uppermost fort in Strathspey is at Laggan. It occupies a superb position on the tip of a long promontory ridge which divides the main valley from Strathmashie. The flanks of the promontory fall steeply from the summit to the Spey's flood plain nearly 600 feet below. Approach to the fort is only reasonably easy along the spine from the south-west. The structure conforms to the shape of the crag and measures some 460 feet by 260 feet within a wall which, as it hugs the uneven contours of the rocky outcrops, varies in width from 13 feet to 23 feet. In some places the faces are exposed to a height of up to 9 feet, revealing that the wall is built of great numbers of rather small coursed stones. This fort is known as Dun Da Lamh (the Fort of the Two Hands) and is reckoned to be the most perfect relic of a British stronghold of the Pictish era to be found in the country. An old iron smelt was discovered near the summit of the Dun, with remains of ashes which showed evidence of heat far greater than can usually be obtained in a blacksmith's forge, a point which has raised interesting speculations among archaeologists. But it may simply have been a very busy smith's forge constantly engaged in the business of making iron weapons for a large fighting force.

The fort at Avielochan, about two and a half miles north of Aviemore, is a strong stone-walled building occupying a rocky promontory on the west side of Strathspey above Loch Vaa. The eastern part of the rock is being quarried and its surface is clothed with a jungle of juniper which is virtually impenetrable. The approach to the fort from the foot of Beinn Ghuilbin takes the form of a narrow neck which is traversed by a high fence erected in recent times to restrict the movement of deer. Just beyond this is the first of a series of ruined walls formed from massive boulders. The next line of defence is a wall, mostly represented by a form of terracing, which girdles the promontory at a level of some 20 feet below the summit. The last line to be encountered is another ruinous wall which encloses an area of juniper-chocked summit which measures about 220 feet long and 80 feet wide. These two forts are prime indications that, at a time just before recorded history, the Spey valley was of particular economic and military importance, with an inference of a fairly large population which required to be protected from incursions and raids by land-hungry neighbours.

The Aviemore area alone has four megalithic stone circles. Much older than the fortifications, they were erected around 2000 B.C., and can be seen at Granish, about two miles north of Aviemore, in a field just north of the Public Hall, and a third at Deflour, about four and a half miles south of the village. These are ring cairns: a number of monoliths in a single, or sometimes double, circle, surrounding an open area with a cairn at the centre. A passage grave structure can be seen near Avielochan, with a tumulus of some 40 feet in diameter. This site is unusual in that it has no accompanying ring of standing stones.

Jumping a number of centuries ahead, there is another indication of the importance of the Spey valley. This is the oldest road in Strathspey of which there is any record: the Via

Regia, the King's Road, or sometimes called Alexander's Road, because it is said to have been constructed on the orders of a Scottish king by the name of Alexander, most likely Alexander II. The date of the making of the road is given as 1263. Alexander II was concerned in repelling Norse raids by the Jarls of Orkney, and it was perhaps natural that a direct route to the north was highly desirable for the movement of defensive troops to prevent the Norse moving south. The road came from the south, over the Drumochter Pass and kept to the right bank of the Spey past Rothiemurchus and Pityoulish to the neighbourhood of Achgourish. There it branched off through Tulloch, south of Staor-na-mannach, which is still called in Gaelic Rathad an Righ, the King's Road. The road was by law endowed with a right of way and pasturage so that it could be used for peaceful as well as military traffic.

In later centuries there was a type of traffic in Strathspey which was not particularly welcomed by the inhabitants: reiving or cattle lifting. This activity consisted simply in stealing cattle from farms and crofts and herding them away to the south along what became known as Thieves' Roads. One of the most important of these routes was the Rathad nam Mearlaich which stretched from Lochaber in the west to the east coast. Its route, cutting across Strathspey, can be traced along the hills of Rothiemurchus by the south side of Loch Morlich and to An Lochan Uaine, better known as the Green Loch. From there it skirted Ryvoan and went across the valley of the River Nethy until the Thieves' Pass was reached between Carn na Loinne and Carn na h-Ailig to reach the ford across the Dorback Burn. Other fording places were used, one in particular, some three miles north of Inchrory, was where "information was distributed regarding the movements of the military patrols; and stolen cattle and horses were hidden in the surrounding country". Towards the height of the Lairig Ghru Pass there is a Thieves' Burn. The name Lairig Laoidh, over the shoulder of Bynack More (3574 feet), indicates another route where there was at some time considerable movement of livestock. In the course of time, these thieves' roads became the drovers' roads, over which cattle were legitimately moved to markets in the south to be sold for the benefit of their rightful owners.

That the valley of the Spey attracted the early missionaries of the old Celtic Church, is evidenced by the many old religious sites in Strathspey. The main centres of settlement included Rothiemurchus, Duthil, Kincardine, Abernethy, Inverallan, Congash, Cromdale, Inveravon, and Knockando. One of the oldest church sites is situated at the bend in the Spey at Inverallan; it is thought to be one of the oldest historical place-names in Strathspey. Many old roads made their way to this site, indicating its importance to the inhabitants of the surrounding countryside. The first cell or church is said to have been established by a St Figgat sometime around A.D.600 There is a St Figgat's Well nearby and at one time in the past there used to be held annually a St Figgat's Fair. Later, the site was passed from the ownership of the Celtic Church to the Roman Church. The church of Inverallan was granted by Walter de Moravia to the Bishop of Moray in the middle of the thirteenth century. Nothing of the old church now remains except the old churchyard, which is frequently flooded by the Spey. There is a predominance of Grant surnames here, indicating the density of that clan which became prominent in the district when the lands of Inverallan were disposed to a Grant of Stratherrick in 1316.

The church at Alvie, sited on a promontory of Loch Alvie, is interesting because of the remains of 150 bodies found in October 1880 beneath the floor of the church, when alterations were being made to the structure of the building. Not even local tradition gives an indication of who these people were. Suggestions have been put forward that the bodies were the tragic outcome of some battle. The skeleton bones, all found lying head to head, were subsequently interred in the churchyard and marked with a stone: "Buried here are the Remains of 150 Human Bodies Found, October 1880, Beneath the Floor of this Church. Who they were, When they Lived, how they Died, Tradition Notes Not". The site is attributed

The tourists come to Aviemore (*above*) to use the Cairngorm chair-lift and (*below*) with caravans.

(*Above*) Every facility at the Aviemore Centre though (*below*) there is peace and quiet by the Spey a hundred yards away.

The Spey at Boat of Garten and (*below*) near Nethybridge.

Grantown-on-Spey
The Spey Bridge of 1931
outside Grantown.

Fishing near Grantown and (*below*) the Spey at Gortons, between Grantown and Craigellachie.

The river between Grantown and Craigellachie.

Tomintoul and (*below*) Tormore Distillery.

The distillery at Knockando and (*below*) its still house.

to St Drostan, with a date of 1380 for the chapel built on the site of an earlier religious cell. The old Lairds of Dunachton were always buried here.

The old church of Kingussie is another ancient religious site. Few details of the church are available earlier than the twelfth century. About the middle of that century, Muriach, the historical Parson of Kingussie, on the death of his brother without issue, became head of his family, and succeeded to the Chiefship of Clan Chattan. He obtained a dispensation from the Pope of the time and subsequently married a daughter of the Thane of Cawdor, by whom he had five sons; surnames about this time having become hereditary, Mac-pherson (son of the parson) became the distinguishing clan name. The village of Kingussie occupies the precincts of the ancient priory, built by George, Earl of Huntly, about 1490 on the site of the old Church of St Columba erected around A.D.565 Other churchyards in Kingussie include Cladh Padhair (Peter) and Cladh Brighde (Bridget), outside Newtonmore, all with very old associations.

St Bride's graveyard, Cladh Brighde, on the banks of the River Calder, has an interesting place in Scotland's legal history. It is but a generation or so since Gaelic was the everyday language of Upper Strathspey; however, various agencies militated against the use of the language until today when it is spoken only by a few. Yet, in all of Speyside, there is one visible piece of evidence here that Gaelic was a vital factor in the life of the communities hereabouts. This is a signpost in Gaelic pointing the way to St Bride's burial ground. For many centuries this last resting place was used by the inhabitants of Newtonmore district, until, in 1875, the tenant of Banchor Farm barricaded the way to the cemetery and, with the approval of his feudal superior, began to build a farm-steading across the roadway itself. This brought the inevitable storm of protest which was ignored; ultimately the protection of the law was sought. An action was raised in the Edinburgh Court of Sessions by Peter Cattanach, a lawyer who had local connections; he lodged a plea for suspension and interdict. The demands were quite reasonable. The plaintiffs did not require the destruction of the new buildings, but asked for an access road to the cemetery, with permanent rights of way to be made from the highway to the burial ground. A legal battle then ensued with the case being brought before the Lords Ordinary who decided that the local folk had a case. The outcome was that the latter got rather more than their original request for simple access. Not only were they to be given their rights of access to Cladh Brighde, but the road was to be constructed at the expense of the respondent. Instead of a footpath, a proper road was to be made to a uniform width of 12 feet and to be maintained with a surface fit for the passage of vehicles. Finally, to ensure that no future encroachment should be made upon local rights, a public notice was required to be erected. This notice can still be seen, just to the east of Calder Bridge. It reads: "An Rathad Daingnichte le Lach. Gu Cladh Bhrighde (The Roadway Established by Law. To St Bride's Graveyard)." The notice is a silent public witness which demonstrates how common rights may be enforced by law against would-be usurpation, and it serves, too, as an interesting memorial to the language which has now all but gone from the daily life and living of Strathspey.

The parish church of St Adamnan, reputed to be of Columban foundation, stands on a high knoll above Loch Insch over the Spey from the village of Kincraig. This old ruined parish church of Rothiemurchus has a walled burying ground; it is isolated in the woods of the Dune Estate which slope down to the Spey. In this place there is to be found the grave of Seath Mor Sgorfhiaclach, a victor in the battle which took place at the North Inch, Perth, in 1396; it is marked by five small stones. The stones are said to have been brought from the prehistoric mound at the Doune, and with them came a prophecy that anyone who removed even one of the stones would die. One man did so and on his way home the River Spey went into a sudden spate and he was drowned while crossing. He was a footman of the Duke of Bedford, who took it upon himself to convince the natives that their superstitious fears were groundless. His grave is to be seen in the same churchyard. After his drowning, the locals were convinced that his death, "drowned while bathing" as his stone's inscription has it, was the direct result of his interference with the stones on Big Shaw's grave. At a later date two other men challenged fate and moved the stones; they too died within the year of their temptation. The first service to be held in the old Dune Parish Church for more than forty years took place in 1977. Before that, some months of hard work went into the restoration of the building as part of a Job Creation Scheme. It is the intention to have a special service every summer to keep the building alive as a church. Some of the old furnishings, including the lectern and the eighteenth-century pewter communion plate are used in a new lease of life after a lapse of time since 1931.

The isolated white parish church of Garten and Kincardine stands on a knoll among fields near Croftmore. By tradition it was dedicated to St Tomhaldaidh. In the fifteenth century a massacre of Cummings (Comyns) by Stewarts and Grants took place within the church itself. The site of the building was used for some fourteen centuries and, despite it being only four miles from the bustle of the Aviemore holiday complex, the old church is seldom visited. Happily, it retains the atmosphere of an earlier time. Inserted into the east gable is a lepers' window, which allowed afflicted persons to watch Mass being said without infecting the rest of the congregation. Outside the door lies the original granite font, probably dating back to the seventh century and thrown out by zealous Reformers at the time of the Reformation in Scotland. The interior design of the building is that of the austere Scottish kirk and the only concession to the weaknesses of the flesh is a huge cast-iron stove in the middle of the floor; lighting is by means of wall-mounted oil lamps.

In the graveyard is a memorial stone to Robert Stewart, grandson of King Robert III, whose descendants held the Barony of Kincardine for several centuries. Also interesting are the number of gravestones erected by sons and relatives in every part of the world to those they left behind. Kincardine was once the centre of a heavily populated district; the hillsides around are dotted with the foundations of abandoned farms and cottages. On the grassed banks outside the graveyard grow dwarf alders, found nowhere else in Strathspey. The tradition concerning their arrival goes back to the time when a daughter of Cameron of Lochiel married the Laird of Kincardine and requested that she be buried in her native soil. When she died a cart was sent from Lochaber with earth. As it arrived at the church some soil spilled onto the bank of the road and the alder seeds took root. They are known locally as 'the Barony Lady's Flowers'.

As in other parts of the Highlands certain clan names predominate in Strathspey and Badenoch; one need only make a tour of the churchyards in different places in the valley to find out which districts were the jealously-guarded territory of one clan or another. There are several traditions regarding the origins of the Grants, who still own large tracts of Speyside. They were thought to be of Anglo-Norman stock and tended to remain a family of little influence until the fifteenth century, when a Great married the heiress of the Lord of Clencharnie, who was a cadet of the Earls of Strathearn who owned lands in Strathspey. Her son, who inherited, first appears as a landholder in 1453; his estates consisted of Glencharnie (largely covered by the present parish of Duthil) and of half of the Barony of Freuchie. A descendant of his built a castle there in 1536 which was afterwards called Bellachastle or Castle Grant. By the end of the sixteenth century the Laird of Freuchie was being styled Laird of Grant or Grant of that Ilk. By the purchase of large tracts of land in Strathspey over a period of the next two centuries, the Grants emerged as a major clan influence. The local people who found themselves beholden to the Grants for their land and work gradually changed their names to that of Grant. Patronymics were generally used in the Highlands at one time, but it was also customary for the tenants, or followers of a chief, to take his surname in order to identify themselves with his family. That this is so is indicated in a list of the parishioners of Duthil dated 1527 in which all the names are Gaelic patronymics. In another list dated 1569, there are nearly fifty names, all Grant. The Grants were, by and large, good chiefs and their existence and influence were of particular value to the common folk on many occasions. The Grants often provided capital for agricultural improvements and gave employment on their estates. In times of scarcity, right down to the nineteenth century, the Laird of Grant imported seed-corn and foodstuffs for his people.

When the Macgregors were deprived of their lands, forbidden to carry arms and had their names proscribed, heavy fines were imposed on anyone who helped a Macgregor in any way. The Lairds of Grant were given many commissions for the collection of these fines and to hunt down the unfortunate Macgregors, but did little about the matter. Indeed, in sharp contrast to the Earls of Argyll, the Grants, chiefs and commoners, were constantly admonished by the Privy Council in Edinburgh for harbouring Macgregors. This is the reason for the many appearances of Rob Roy Macgregor in Strathspey and the rather special relationship between the two clans is one of the better of the aspects in Highland clan history.

One instance indicates the strength of the relationship. South of Coylumbridge and crossing the River Druie is Iron Bridge (the Cairngorm Club footbridge) not far from Allt Druie where there is an open meadow which even today shows signs of past crofting activity. The community here had an association with Rob Roy Macgregor. In the sixteenth century the Shaws held Rothiemurchus. When Allan Shaw, their chief, was outlawed for having murdered his stepfather he was dispossessed of his lands which were then purchased by the Chief of Grant, or rather he bought the right to hold the estate and pass it on to his second son, Patrick Grant (1570). However, this only led to an increase in the bitter fighting between the Shaws and the Grants. The Shaws, in their struggle, enlisted the help of the Chief of Mackintosh, who was in fact, the Shaws' chieftain and so the in-fighting continued for years with no gain on either side. About a century later another Patrick Grant, grandson of the first-named, was the Laird of Rothiemurchus, known as Macalpine, a clan related to the Macgregors with whom he was on very friendly terms. The feud between the Grants and the Shaws carried on apace until the Mackintosh set up a mill outside the western boundary of Rothiemurchus and announced his intention of diverting water from Rothiemurchus to run the mill. Macalpine naturally objected, but only got a threat to have his lands devastated by burning. So Patrick sent a messenger to ask Rob Roy Macgregor for his help. The latter duly arrived from Balquidder, a distance of over 100 miles, with a band of men. The Mackintosh, now realizing his own safety was in danger, duly withdrew from the confrontation and had his mill burnt to the ground. This is said to be the origin of the Black Mill at the entrance to Glen Feshie. Rob Roy then returned to Balquidder but left behind two of his men to act as messengers should further trouble arise. A small spot of bother then cropped up when one of the Macgregors eloped with one of Patrick Grant's daughters, a union to which Grant, for all his friendship with the Macgregors, was opposed. But in the end he relented and gave the couple the croft lands of Allt Druie, the ruins of which can still be seen. The last Macgregor of Allt Druie died in 1890.

During the Forty-five, the Grants were on the side of the Government, and they met with a half-hearted response when they asked their clansmen to support the Royalist cause, for many of the commoner Grants had Jacobite sympathies. Indeed, some of the cadet families of the Grants, for example those in Glenmoriston in the Great Glen, actually joined the Jacobites. Ludovick Grant, the then Chief, acted as the least worthy member of his long line, for he hunted down Jacobite fugitives, often with tragic results. He once took over the surrender of more than eighty men from Glenurquhart and Glenmoriston and handed them over unconditionally to the Duke of Cumberland. These men had surrendered under the impression that they would not be harmed by the law, save lightly, for their support of the Jacobite cause. In the event, they were shipped to London and, without fair trial, sent to Barbados. By 1749 only eighteen men had survived the brutal treatment they received and a mere seven men were eventually able to return home. The Laird of Grant's losses and expenses in the Forty-five were estimated at £20,000 for which he received no compensation. Perhaps this was a just reward. It was James Grant who founded the town of Grantown on Spey in 1766. By 1837 a son of his, Francis, had planted nearly 32 million trees on the Grant lands, a continuing process which has given Strathspey its distinctive character, even today after centuries of tree-felling.

The history of Clan Grant tends to be somewhat less eventful than that of many other Highland clans; rather it is one of steady consolidation of their landholdings, mainly by purchase, than by force of arms. The territory of the clan is especially associated with Strathspey: the thirty miles or so between the two Craigellachies – from Aviemore, where the Spey passes from the uplands of Badenoch, to where, its course all but run, the Spey enters the coastal plain of Moray. The clan battle cry is "Craigellachie", the eminence standing above Aviemore. The three crowns in the Grant coat of arms is said to have been given to an ancestor by the kings of the three Scandinavian kingdoms. Another tradition insists that the Grants can trace their descent from the ancient Kings of Alba, through the Macgregors. Highland oral tradition being in the main consistent, this might be more than likely, considering the special relationships of the Grants with the Macgregors, particularly during the troubled period of the latter clan.

The Shaws and the Cummings (Comyns) had a more chequered history, both being involved in struggles for power and supremacy in medieval times, with dark deeds done by one to the other until they went into decline as a major influence in Strathspey. One example of the relationship between the two clans is recorded in tradition. At the eastern end of Loch Pityoulish there is a spot on which no plant will grow except the blueberry. It was here, centuries ago, that a contingent of Comyns was wiped out by the Shaws, who were, in their heyday, Lords of Rothiemurchus. The dead Comyns were interred at the spot and accounts for nothing but their clan plant being able to grow to commemorate the dead.

The clan territory of the Comyns was Badenoch and the chiefs were know as the Lords of Badenoch. The family rose to prominence in the twelfth century to become the Earls of Buchan by marriage. John, the Red Comyn, was one of the six guardians of Scotland during the minority of the Maid of Norway and later became one of the competitors for the Crown of Scotland. Another member, known as the Black Comyn, was, like so many other nobles, known for his self-interest and fought alternately for and against Scotland until he was stabbed to death by Robert the Bruce at Dumfries in 1306. The line died with the death of John Comyn in 1325, since when the direct line ceased to exist as he left no heirs; the family is now represented by the Cummings of Altyre. A member of this family was Roualeyn Gordon-Cumming, the famous traveller and lion-hunter of last century.

The Clan Shaw was one of the principal clans of Clan Chattan. As a result of the clan chief's participation in the battle on the North Inch, Perth in 1396, Shaw Mor was given Rothiemurchus. But the lands were sold in the sixteenth century. The clan supported Montrose in the seventeenth century and were later involved in the Jacobite Rising of 1715. A new chief of Clan Shaw, the twenty-first, matriculated his arms in 1970 after a vacancy of 400 years.

Badenoch is the country of the Clan Chattan, among whom are included the Macphersons and the Mackintoshes. The Clan Chattan (the Clan of the Cats) was an ancient political confederation of Highland clans which also included Davidsons, MacBeans, Farquharsons and MacGillivrays. The first Captain of Clan Chattan was Angus, sixth Laird of Mackintosh, but the chiefs of Clan Macpherson claimed this title on the grounds that they were descended from Muireach, the Parson of Kingussie who, in 1173 was also Chief of Clan Chattan. For some two centuries the two clans feuded over the chiefship. In 1672 Cluny Macpherson matriculated arms as "the laird of Cluny and the only true representer of the ancient and honourable family of Clan Chattan", but the Chief of Mackintosh protested and the arms given to Cluny were withdrawn and given instead new arms as a cadet of Clan Chattan.

The Gaelic name of Macpherson is MacMhuirich, denoting their descent from Muriach, Parson of Kingussie. In the emergence of the clan, various families of Macphersons jockeyed for .power, a state of affairs which ended when the family of Cluny emerged as the most important. One of the main names in the family history is that of Ewen Macpherson of Cluny who, during the Forty-five, raised 600 men to join the Jacobite cause. They behaved with gallantry on many occasions but arrived too late at Culloden battlefield to share in the fighting and the defeat. After Culloden, Cluny actively assisted Prince Charles, for which fidelity to the cause, Cluny's house was burnt to the ground and he himself had to go into hiding in Badenoch for some nine years. Despite a reward of £1000 on his head, he was never captured or betrayed and he ultimately escaped to France in 1755. The Cluny estates were then forfeited but were restored in 1784 to Duncan Macpherson, son of Ewen. The Clan Museum at Newtonmore is full of interest and displays many items of clan history.

The Davidsons, another Badenoch clan claim descent from David Dubh of Invernahavon, who went under the umbrella of the Clan Chattan Federation as a means of protecting his family and small band of adherents. The clan was represented at the Battle of North Inch in Perth from which only one man survived at the termination of the combat. After that disaster the clan went into obscurity and Davidson as a Strathspey surname became rare.

The clan name of Mackintosh is derived from the Gaelic Mac an Toisich, son of the chief. The founder of the clan is by tradition a son of MacDuff, an ancestor of the Earls of Fife.

The Mackintoshes were one of the two principal clans forming the Clan Chattan Federation. The rise of the clan to prominence was accompanied by feuds with the Earls of Moray and Huntly and such clans as Macpherson, Cameron, Gordon and MacDonell of Keppoch. In 1639 when the Earl of Huntly supported the King, Mackintosh joined the Covenanting side north of the Spey and later formed part of the army which opposed Cromwell in 1650. The clan was prominent in the Jacobite Rising of 1715. In the Forty-five Angus Mackintosh the chief was on the side of the Government, while his wife, Anne, who was a Farquharson of Invercauld, raised the clan standard for Prince Charles. Her strategy was responsible for the Rout of Moy, when 1500 Government troops were put to flight by half a dozen of the lady's retainers. The chiefships of Clan Chattan and Clan Mackintosh were separated in 1938 on the death of the 28th Chief of Mackintosh.

History pops up in some odd and unexpected corners as the River Spey makes its way north. When King James VI was succeeded by his son, Charles I, in 1625, Scotland came in for a bad time of it. His father had had an intimate knowledge of his native country, whereas the son was quite unfamiliar with his northern kingdom. While his father had preached, but rarely practised, the absolute authority of the monarch, Charles I believed in it as a religion. The result was a build-up of conflict between the King and the Scottish Church and nobility. In 1638 the National Covenant was circulated throughout Scotland for approval, designed to declare to the King that at all costs, the Scots were willing to resist prelacy by restoring Presbyterianism on a pure and simple basis. But armed force was needed to uphold these wishes, and alignments began to be formed between the two factions. By 1640 the Covenanters were in control in Scotland, a grasp which was only to be ruptured by the advent of the Solemn League and Covenant (1643) by which Covenanters agreed to assist the parliamentary opposition to Charles I in England, in return for the security of their own regime in Scotland. The agreement was denounced by Montrose who made a brilliant but unsuccessful attempt to win his countrymen back in support of the King and the original aims of the National Covenant.

A series of military campaigns in Scotland were left in the air by 1649, when the troubled career of Charles I came to an end with his trial and execution by his English opponents. Charles II was then proclaimed King in Edinburgh, in February 1649, and negotiations were opened with him in exile at The Hague. Ambassadors were sent to The Hague to offer him, as the price for the Scottish Crown, certain conditions which were known to be repugnant to him. Months of wrangling followed until Montrose landed with a force of 1200 men in Orkney and in the north of Scotland, to meet with nothing but disaster. In the meantime Charles II had accepted to be a 'Covenanted King', and with this in mind he set out from Holland for Scotland. The commander of the Dutch frigate bearing the royal personage was none other than Cornelis Tromp, the son of the famous Dutch admiral who was such a thorn in the side of the English navy, and was popularly believed to have carried a broom at his masthead as a sign of his ability to sweep the English from the seas. The frigate was convoyed to the mouth of the River Spey, with two other ships carrying the King's retinue.

The 23rd June saw the King's ship lying off-shore at Kingston-on-Spey. As his ship could not come close inshore, His Majesty was carried to dry land on the back of a Kingston native named Milne, whose descendants were ever afterwards called the King's Milnes, the last of whom died in 1885. On shore was a large number of Scots nobles, waiting for the King to put his signature to the historic Solemn League and Covenant. The signing took place at a house in Kingston on whose walls is fixed a plaque commemorating the event. After signing, Charles was subjected to "notable sermons and exhortations made unto him by the ministers", to whom, no doubt he listened with great impatience.

Charles then made his way south, having swallowed the Covenant like a nauseous pill, and was crowned at Scone on

1st January 1651, after which he took to the field at the head of an army of 20,000 men to dispute the pretensions of Oliver Cromwell. But within a year Charles found himself on the Continent once more and had to wait until 1660 before he was restored to the throne and crowned in some triumph at Westminster.

In the minds of many people, that event in Scottish, if not British, history known as the Forty-five was a short-lived episode. However, the truth is that while the ultimate child of the Jacobite hopes in the British Isles was indeed short-lived, it was a long time in its fostering. The time of its birth was 1688, when James III and VIII of the Jacobites, known as the Old Pretender, was born in St James's Palace. When William of Orange landed, and Revolution was about to break out, the young prince and his mother were sent to France. James II, his father, left England afterwards to spend the rest of his life in the Château of St Germain-en-Laye, near Paris, where he died in 1701. In 1705 there appeared the first in a long line of plots: the Scots Plot, engineered by Simon Fraser, the Lord Lovat, whose scandalous conduct in 1702 had brought him before the courts to be outlawed for a criminal outrage. Fleeing to France, he hatched out his scheme and persuaded King Louis XIV of France to support a military expedition to Scotland. The main force was to land at Dundee and then go westwards to capture Fort William and open up the way for the clans to join the cause for the restoration of the Stuarts to the throne of Britain. But things went wrong, with betrayal and mistrust an outstanding feature of the venture. Lovat went back to France and was kept in tight confine for many years. But it was this plot which firmly equated the Highlanders with Jacobitism, Lovat having painted the willingness of the clan chiefs and their followers to support any attempt to restore the former order of things. There was a reason for his doing this, for at that time the Highlanders were the only inhabitants of Great Britain who had retained the habit of the use of arms. While the Scots Plot had little effect in Scotland, it had a lasting influence in France and it reacted on all future projects of Jacobite action, for Lovat's account of the fighting quality of the Highlanders had been so impressive that it became, in the ensuing decades, quite unthinkable for any action to be taken without the inclusion of Highlanders.

Another attempt at a military expedition took place in 1708, a year after the Treaty of Union of 1707 was forced upon an unwilling Scottish population. The political times were ripe, it was thought, and a squadron of ships and a small army was equipped for an invasion. But the characteristic ill-luck of the Stuarts struck, with the Old Pretender falling ill, and this delayed the scheme. Shortly afterwards the British Government learned of the plot and made some defensive preparations. The French expedition carrying James left to land in the Firth of Forth; but the admiral in charge of the fleet missed his bearings and found himself at Montrose. He retraced his wakes and anchored close to the Isle of May in the Forth, where he had to engage British ships. He then fled north where, within sight and sound of the Scottish coastline, James implored to be set down. But the admiral refused and took the old king back to France, the latter with little but a visual contact with the shores of his lost kingdom.

Then came the rising of 1715. This began at Braemar in September of that year, to be followed by the English rising in Northumberland. The latter movement was crushed at Preston in November, on the same day as the indecisive battle was fought at Sherriffmuir in Perthshire. King James landed at Peterhead in December from whence he went to Perth to establish his Court at the ancient royal palace of Scone. There he was proclaimed King and exercised regal functions. But he had arrived too late. He had been assured that the whole of the kingdom was on his side; instead, he met with dissension and discontent. He left Scotland in February 1716, found that France was unwilling to accept him as an exile, and eventually found refuge at Urbino, in Italy, in the Papal States.

Another attempt to further the Jacobite cause was made in 1719, this time with the help of Spain. An armada was to carry a Spanish army to the west of England, while a smaller force was to land in north-western Scotland. Both expeditions sailed away to meet nothing but misfortune. The larger force was dispersed by a storm; the smaller force, unaware of this turn of events, landed in the north-west Highlands. After some vicissitudes, the Scottish end of the venture ended at the Battle of Glenshiel, when the Spanish troops surrendered.

Prince Charles Edward was born in 1720, an event which gave the Jacobites renewed hope and fresh vigour for further plots, the final grand slam being the Forty-five, a rising which was to involve Strathspey in a number of rather interesting ways. The first association of the rising with the area was when news reached the Jacobites that Sir John Cope and his troops had reached Dalwhinnie and was preparing to march over the Corrieyairack Pass to gain the safety of Fort Augustus. A party of Jacobites were sent into the pass to hold it and prevent this manoeuvre. Cope, in his turn, on hearing the pass was being held to prevent him gaining a foothold in the Great Glen, decided to head north and make for Inverness. The Jacobites then made a raid on the barracks at Ruthven with an intent on its destruction; but they were beaten off by the inmates with some losses. The next time Ruthven saw the Jacobites was in February of the following year, 1746, when they were retreating north after the turn-around at Derby; they burnt the barracks to render it unfit for military use. The third and last time Ruthven was to see the Prince's army was on 18th April 1746, two days after the defeat at Culloden. It was here that the message was received from the Prince, thanking his friends for their bravery and devotion and desiring them to do what they thought best for their own preservation; the army then dispersed to the hills for safety.

Thereafter followed some desperate months for the Prince and his scattered followers. The Prince found himself in Badenoch in August 1746, a month before he finally escaped from Scotland to France. He stayed in what is known as Cluny's Cage (a cave on Ben Alder, by Loch Ericht) with Cameron of Lochiel, Cluny Macpherson and some others, for about a week until news arrived that French ships were in the vicinity of Loch nan Uamh, when he left for his own safety.

The cave was located high on a southern spur of Ben Alder. It consisted of a shanty in a thicket of hollies. It had two floors and was covered with moss as a thatch. The upper room served as a dining and bedroom and the lower used to store supplies. As a contemporary MS describes it: "At the back part was a proper hearth for cook and baiker, and the face of the mountain had so much the colour and resemblance of smoke, no person could ever discover that there was either fire or habitation in the place. Round this lodge were placed their sentinels at proper stations, some nearer and some at greater distances."

Near Laggan is Cluny Castle, which stands on the site of the old home of the Macpherson chiefs. In 1745 Ewen Macpherson, chief of the Clan Macpherson, was appointed to a company in Lord Loudon's Highlanders, on the side of the Government. But on the arrival of Prince Charles, he threw up his commission and, with 600 Macphersons, joined the Prince after the latter's victory at Prestonpans. In the retreat from Derby, the clan greatly distinguished themselves, especially by their gallantry in the skirmish with Government troops at Clifton. Lord George Murray commanded on that occasion, with Cluny at the head of his men. Exasperated at the volley of fire from the opposition, Cluny took claymore in hand and charged the enemy lines, followed by his clansmen, and thoroughly dispersed them. The clan arrived too late to take part in the battle of Culloden, though they formed the first line at the Battle of Falkirk.

After Culloden, Government troops devastated the Highlands, and the property of those who had 'come out' for the Jacobite cause came in for particular attention. Cluny Castle was burnt to the ground and the chief's family had to go into hiding. Ewen Macpherson had a price of £1000 on his head. But the same faithful and loyal spirit which had induced Highlanders not to betray the whereabouts of Prince Charles Edward for £30,000, also protected Cluny for some eight years until he managed to effect an escape to France. He lived for much of the time in Cluny's Cave (not to be confused with the Cage mentioned earlier). This hiding place was a cave located high in the steep and rocky face of Creag Dubh, a hill which rises some 2350 feet above the River Spey. It is from this hill that the Macphersons derive their battle cry of "Creag Dubh". The cave is difficult of access and to locate. The faithful clansmen in 1746 improved conditions in the cave by some excavation to form two rooms. This work they did at night and before dawn all rubble had been thrown into the Spey's waters. Cluny had many narrow escapes. On one occasion he was in a house paying a quick visit to his family when a party of redcoats surrounded the building. With great presence of mind, Cluny dressed himself in the clothes of a servant, went outside and offered to hold the officer's horse. The offer was accepted and Cluny walked the horse about while the house was being searched for him. On the officer's return, Cluny held his stirrup and received a shilling for his trouble and attention.

Cluny escaped to France in 1755 and died at Dunkirk the following year, his time in hiding having proved too much for his constitution. The search for this brave Highland chief brought another famous name on to the Strathspey stage: that of General James Wolfe, of the Heights of Abraham.

The General stayed at Fort Augustus after the Forty-five. His task was to ensure that Jacobites were not encouraged in any way to repeat their performance in 1745. His reputation as a humane soldier stood him in good stead, as distinct from that of General Hawley, the Hanging General, whose name stank in the nostrils of both Jacobite and Government forces. Wolfe had gone to Fort Augustus in 1752 after a spell of duty on the Continent, and found the countryside peaceful enough. Perhaps the atrocities committed under the orders of the Duke of Cumberland after Culloden had struck fear into the clans. It was while there Wolfe heard news of the famous Appin Murder:

"You may have heard," he wrote to his father, "of the strange murder that was committed about a fortnight since by two Highlanders, at the instigation, it is believed, of a lady, the wife of a banished rebel. The gentleman was an Argyllshire man, and factor upon some of the forfeited estates. Several men are apprehended upon suspicion, but I'm sure it will be very difficult to discover the actors of this bloody deed. The factor intended to remove the old tenants and to plant others in their room, and this is supposed to be the reason for killing him."

While at Fort Augustus, one of Wolfe's tasks was the capture of Cluny Macpherson, who, since 1746, had been living often within sight of his home, but never certain where he would rest the following night in peace from his persistent hunters. A Captain Trapaud, one of Wolfe's senior officers, was detailed to command the post at Laggan. The Captain set out with a detachment to try to run Cluny down. "I gave orders," Wolfe wrote years after the event, "(in case he should succeed) and was attacked by the Clan with a view to rescue him their chief to kill him instantly, which I concluded would draw on the destruction of the Detachment and furnish me with sufficient pretext (without waiting for any instructions) to march into their country *ou j'aurais fait main basse, sans misericorde, et je l'aurais brûlé d'un bout à l'autre* [on which I shall lay violent hands, without mercy, and I shall burn it from one extremity to the other]. Would you believe that I am so bloody? 'Twas my real intention, and I hope such execution will be done upon that first revolt, to teach 'em their duty and keep the Highlands in awe. They are a people better govern'd by fear than favour."

For the sake of Wolfe's reputation in Scotland, perhaps it is as well that his attempt to capture Cluny failed, as all earlier, and more ambitious attempts had similarly miscarried.

"Mr Mcpherson shou'd have a couple of hundred men in his neighbourhood, with orders to massacre the whole Clan if they should show the least symptom of rebellion. They are a warlike tribe, and he's a cunning resolute fellow himself. They shou'd be narrowly watch'd; and the Party there shou'd be well commanded." Thus Wolfe wrote in 1755 to his succeeding officer before leaving Fort Augustus, not knowing perhaps that about this time Cluny, weary of playing hide and seek with the Redcoats, had escaped to France, probably carrying with him the remnants of the Loch Arkaig gold.

Of all the historical characters associated with Strathspey, perhaps the Wolf of Badenoch stands out above many; his reputation rests on some of the blackest pages in Scotland's history and in the old traditions in the area. The Wolf of Badenoch was a natural son of King Robert II, and was known as Alasdair Mor mac an Righ, Big Alexander, son of the King. Even in the barbarous days in which he lived he was regarded as a monster and was feared both far and wide. He died in 1394 and is buried at Dunkeld, in Perthshire. In his times he was Lord of Badenoch, Earl of Buchan and his brother's royal Deputy in the north of Scotland. When he deserted his wife, the Countess of Ross, she appealed for redress to the Bishop of Moray, who gave judgement in her favour. Alexander, in reply, seized some of the Bishop's lands and was, in return, excommunicated. In a savage fury, the Wolf of Badenoch, bent on revenge, swooped down from his stronghold castle of Lochindorb and sacked and burned the towns of Forres and Elgin, the latter being the ecclesiastical heart of the bishopric of Moray. He rode with his men into the sleeping town of Elgin one dark night and set off a series of fires, mainly the College and Canon's houses, and the Hospital of the Maison Dieu. The terrified burghers of Elgin fled with their families into the surrounding countryside. Tradition has it that some of these, like Lot's wife, looked back at the sight of the burning Cathedral, with its Gothic windows a tracery of stone against the flames, and were frozen in their tracks with horror. Begun in 1224, the building was one of Scotland's most magnificent structures, and its wanton destruction was unbelievable. Alexander's father called on his son to do penance for his crime at the door of the Church of the Blackfriars in Perth. This, the Wolf of Badenoch did and then, in the presence of his father, the King, nobles and many church dignitaries, the Wolf was finally pardoned and received back into the Church. The cause of all his misdeeds was his absolute refusal to leave his mistress, the Lady Mariota Athyn, and live with his wife the Countess. Mariota, he went to great length to point out, had borne him five sons whereas the Countess brought only her land with too tight a hold on it. The Wolf's repentance was only skin-deep, however, or so tradition has it. One legend concerns his death in 1394. He was visited in Ruthven Castle, where the ruins of the Ruthven Barracks now stand, by a tall man dressed in black who played a game of chess with him.

Hour after hour the game was played until it seemed that time itself was standing still in anticipation of the game's outcome. Suddenly the mysterious visitor moved a piece. "Check", he said; "checkmate", and rose from the game table. His words were accompanied by a clap of thunder, followed by a storm of hail and lightning. The castle was rent through by terrible sounds until the morning, when silence reigned. But in that pall of silence, the Wolf of Badenoch's men were found outside the walls, dead and blackened as though fired by lightning. Of the chief there was no sign; but in the banqueting hall his body was found, unharmed and tidy, save for one feature: all the nails in his boots had been torn out. Two days later a funeral procession was started from the castle; bier after bier was carried out. But no sooner had the last of them been added to the procession when another great storm started; it was concluded that the wrath of the heavens was centred on the coffins. The problem was solved by six strong men taking the Wolf's coffin, which had led the procession, to the rear. No sooner had this been done, when the storm ceased and the procession was able to proceed. After that event, the local people told of seeing weird lights in the castle at night, with the Wolf of Badenoch replaying his last game of chess with the Devil.

The eldest son of the Wolf of Badenoch became Earl of Mar and this title, one of the oldest in Scotland, still survives. In the year 1451 the Lordship of Badenoch passed to the Earl of Huntly, ancestor of the Duke of Gordon, who died in 1836.

Lochindorb Castle, seven miles from Grantown, the favourite haunt of the Wolf, occupies an island in the middle of the loch, which is supposed to be wholly artificial. It is on the quadrilateral plan common with castles of the thirteenth century, with round towers at each corner. The castle belonged to the Comyns of Badenoch in the thirteenth century. In 1303, King Edward I of England led an expedition into the Comyn territory, to reduce them to submission, and captured Lochindorb Castle, residing there for a month. The English forces remained in possession of the castle for a number of years and used their time by adding the outer court to enclose the whole of the island base. Forty years later it became the prison of William Bullock, a favourite of David Bruce, who, being suspected of conniving with the English, was starved to death in its dungeon. In 1335 the Scottish Regent, Sir Andrew Moray, besieged it against the Duke of Atholl, who was holding the structure for Edward Baliol. By the fifteenth century it had become a Douglas stronghold; it was destroyed in 1458 by the Thane of Cawdor by order of King James II. Near the loch is a road supposed to be of Roman origin, but was in fact laid down much later; it is mentioned in a Charter of King Alexander II.

Another castle in a loch is that of Loch an Eilean. Like Lochindorb Castle, which it much resembles in situation, it is a thirteenth-century stronghold and was another important base of the Wolf of Badenoch. The first stage in its construction was undertaken by Lachlan Mackintosh, then Chief of the confederation of clans known as Clan Chattan, which included the Macphersons and the Davidsons. It is first mentioned in 1539 when the lands in the area passed to a Master George Gordon, son of Lord Huntly. Various additions were made to the original structure until it covered the wole island. In 1688 it was defended by the laird's wife, Grizel Mor, when it was attacked by a band of adherents of James II after the battle of Cromdale in that year. Its last use was as a prison in 1745 by the Laird of Rothiemurchus, who shut up some of his tenants to prevent them from taking up arms on behalf of the

Jacobite cause. Its interest now lies mainly in the ospreys which nest in the walls. When the Grants succeeded the Shaws in possession of lands in Strathspey, it was repaired and fortified by Patrick Grant, to give him a base from which he could defend his disputed rights to the lands. About 1520 Lachlan Mackintosh of Dunachton was murdered in the castle by a near kinsman. One account states that three men were responsible for the chief's murder. They were tried and found guilty. One was sentenced to be beheaded and quartered; the other two were punished with slightly less severity, their sentence being that they should be hanged and their heads fixed on poles at the scene of their crime.

Balvenie Castle is on the outskirts of Dufftown. It was in its time one of the largest castles in the north of Scotland. Despite its age it is in an excellent state of preservation. This moated stronghold of the fourteenth century was originally owned by the Comyn family. It was visited with intent and purpose by Edward I of England in 1303. It then passed into the hands of the Black Douglasses and in 1460 to the Stewart Earls of Athole. Its disturbed history continued during the wars of the seventeenth century; it was occupied by the Duke of Cumberland's troops in 1746.

Castle Grant, near Grantown was once named Freuchie. For some six centuries it was the home of the chiefs of Clan Grant, ever since Sir John Grant received, in the thirteenth century, a gift from the King of the Scots of part of the lands of Strathspey formerly held by the Comyns. It was first named Castle Grant in 1694. The towers of the castle are the oldest parts of the building, dating from c. 1200. One of the towers is reputed to be haunted by the ghost of Lady Barbara, or Barbie, who was walled up alive here for her misdeeds. The castle was the home of the Chiefs of Grant, the Earls of Seafield, but the seventh Earl and his son, who succeeded him, broke the entail and the eighth Earl, who died in 1884, left the estates to his mother. Since then there have been landless chiefs of Grant and Earls of Seafield.

Now empty, Castle Grant was once a focal point of interest

and had many famous visitors in its days. Queen Victoria, in her *Journal*, described the castle as "a very plain-looking house, like a factory". In 1618 it was visited by John Taylor, the 'Penniless Poet', who anticipated modern sensation-mongering by making a tour of the British Isles with empty pockets and wrote up his observations for the gossip-reading fraternity of his time. Robert Burns was a guest in the castle, where he met the 'Bonnie Lesley', whom he later immortalized in song. During the Forty-five, the castle fell into the hands of the Jacobites who occupied it for some days, but did no damage apart from consuming some of the welcome stores they found in the cellars.

From a distance, the ruins of Ruthven Castle, or more correctly, Ruthven Barracks, are nothing if not imposing. Standing on a mound, the present ruins are what is left of the fortification destroyed by the Jacobites in 1746. The mound, however, has had a structure on it for ages. It was a base of power of the mighty Comyns, then Lords of Badenoch; later it was the main stronghold of the Gordons, the latter having bought the Lordship of Badenoch from the King in 1452. The Wolf of Badenoch used the castle too when visiting the southern lands of Strathspey. In the sixteenth century a new structure was built only to be demolished later in 1689 by Claverhouse. In 1718 the Government of the day erected on the site a new building to be used as a staging barracks for troops and horses, which managed to survive until the Forty-five. The site at Ruthven has had many famous visitors in its day, including Mary, Queen of Scots, and Cameron of Lochiel and MacDonald of Keppoch, both of whom were imprisoned there in 1546 by the Earl of Huntly. General Wolfe, the Marquis of Montrose and Generals Monk and Wade, all were familiar with Ruthven in one way or another. The barracks built to police the unruly Highland and Jacobite forces after the Fifteen, it fell to the supporters of the same cause thirty years later to demolish the structure, though not completely. When the Jacobites assembled at Ruthven in 1746, immediately after their defeat at Culloden, they expected to carry on the campaign; instead they received the message to disperse, which they did after blowing up the buildings so that they could not be used to house English redcoats. It was not, however, the first encounter the garrison there had had with the Jacobites. In the previous year the barracks were successfully defended against an attack by the Highlanders. The defending party were troops left behind by Sir John Cope when he marched north to Inverness, comprising a sergeant and twelve men. Soon afterwards these men found themselves confronted by a body of 200 Highlanders; they held out, however, and were left in peace – until February 1746 when another attack on the buildings was launched by 300 Jacobites under the command of Gordon of Glenbucket. After a brave defence lasting three days, the inmates surrendered on honourable terms and were allowed to march away, a quite different picture from the events which occurred after Culloden, when even Highland wounded were killed where they lay and those who surrendered voluntarily were killed without delay.

The structure as built in 1718 consisted of two parallel buildings of equal length running nearly east-west, connected by two buildings of lesser height lying in a transverse direction, and all forming a complete square large enough to accommodate two companies of men. There was, besides, a fairly large house which served the purpose of a stable for a number of horses.

One Speyside character who still lives on in the folk-music scene in Scotland is James Macpherson, the freebooter. He was of an illegitimate branch of the family of Macphersons of Invereshie, with his mother a gipsy, or a member of a family of tinkers. He was brought up in his father's house until the latter died, when the boy came under the influence of his mother, who taught him the habits and ideals of her tribe. James was uncommonly intelligent and had a number of talents, including the playing of the violin. In his youth he became the head of a wandering party of freebooters who were notable for their Robin Hood customs of taking from the rich and giving to the poor. As a result, they were an extremely popular bunch of characters among the common folk who, on more than one occasion, effected their escape from custody when they were apprehended. Eventually James Macpherson was caught at a Keith market and lodged in Banff Jail in November 1700. After a trial of sorts, Macpherson and three of his companions were found guilty of numerous charges and sentenced to be hanged. The trial has its place in Scottish legal history as being the last ever to be held under the old laws of Heritable Jurisdiction, under which lairds had the power of 'pit and gallows' over common folk, and also because it produced a death sentence. Invariably, unlike similar cases in England, banishment was the more usual penalty in Scotland; it was the fact of the sentence of death which caused an appeal to be lodged on behalf of Macpherson and his companions.

But the authorities were determined that James Macpherson should die and so contrived that his hanging should take place before the appointed hour. Tradition has it that the town clock was put forward so that the hanging could be carried out before any reprieve might arrive. At the gallows, Macpherson took his parting of this life lightly and defiantly. He played on his violin, a tune now known as "Macpherson's Rant":

> There's some cam' here tae see me hanged
> An some tae buy my fiddle,
> But lang e'er I shall part wi her,
> I'll brak her i' the middle.
>
> He tak the fiddle intae his haun,
>   He's brak it ower a stane,
> "Nae ithir haun shall gar her sing
>   When I am deid an gane!"
>
> Sae rantinly, sae wantonly,
>   Sae dauntonly gaed he –
> He played a tune and he daunced it roun
>   Aneath the gallows-tres.

One version of the tradition of James Macpherson's hanging has it that after he had played, he offered the instrument to anyone in the watching crowd who would accept it. But none dared show any degree of friendship towards him for fear of reprisals against them afterwards, taken by the authorities. So – one could imagine Macpherson's fit of sadness at the ultimate rejection – hĕ broke the instrument and threw it into the crowd. But the pieces were gathered up and they later were passed into the hands of Cluny, chief of the Clan Macpherson. The shattered fiddle can still be seen in the Clan Macpherson Museum at Newtonmore. The ballad celebrating the incident has a number of versions, one being composed by Robert Burns. The tune to which it is sung is supposed to be that played by Macpherson himself. To add a touch of romance to this story, it is said that just after he was hanged, a messenger arrived in Banff with Macpherson's reprieve. But, if that had happened Scots tradition would have been the poorer for the loss.

One James Macpherson firmly fixed in the traditions of his native Strathspey would, one would think, be sufficient. But there is another. In the middle of the eighteenth century, the attention of the educated classes in Europe was brought sharply to bear on a group of poems translated from Gaelic and said to be of the same age as the works of Homer the Greek. These poems were produced by James Macpherson of Kingussie and they brought about a revolution in European literary tradition, the echoes of which are still as vibrant today as they were in 1762. James Macpherson was born in the now derelict hamlet of Ruthven in 1738 and was educated in the village school there, where he was later to become its head-master. He received his higher education at Inverness and at the Universities of Aberdeen and Edinburgh, which he turned to excellent use in his future careers. When he was twenty years of age he published a poem called "The Highlander", which was obscure and based on a mixture of Grecian and Gothic mythology and which, somewhat deservedly, was ignored. However, two years later he presented fragments of ancient Gaelic poetry which caused no end of a stir. While genius shone through the verses, they also bore the stamp of a rhythm only associated with heroic poetry. The result was that a public subscription was raised to enable Macpherson to travel throughout the Highlands and Islands of Scotland to collect other fragments of ancient poetry. In 1762 he presented to the world the results of his mission in *Fingal*, and other poems, which he suggested were composed by Ossian, son of Fingal. The book was a bestseller and its reputation spread like wildfire, not only throughout Britain but Europe.

From *Fingal* there rose the Romantic Movement in European literature which, within a few years, had a great influence on approaches to writing and inspired not a few writers and composers, including Goethe and Wagner, to produce a new kind of literature and music. Napoleon Bonaparte is said to have carried a volume of *Fingal* everywhere on his campaigns, and it was these poems which persuaded him to re-establish the Scots College in Paris, which had been destroyed in the French Revolution. Macpherson was lionized everywhere he went. However, in 1763 a second volume entitled *Temora* made its appearance which, instead of consolidating Macpherson's reputation, had the opposite effect: scholars became suspicious of the authenticity of the poems. When asked to produce the original documents from which he professed to translate the ancient Gaelic poem into English, Macpherson refused. Latter-day research has in fact confirmed that Macpherson had simply made a good job of restoring and re-structuring old Gaelic epic poems. He had claimed, somewhat misguidedly, that the poems were translations. In fact, they were productions which gave the general meanings of the Ossianic verses, told in Macpherson's own words and with additions of his own, which he inserted in order to support his belief that the poems had originally formed part of a single epic, comparable to the *Odyssey*.

Truth is mixed up with fancy here. It has been confirmed within reason that a poet named Ossian did live in the third century A.D. and that the heroes mentioned in *his* works were real people, although many of their deeds were 'written up' to make a good story. Even today, there are tradition-bearers in the Highlands and Islands who can recite Ossian's poems – people who have learned the verses orally, the traditional way. The poems were in fact generally known throughout Scotland, though they survived longest in the Gaelic-speaking areas on the western seaboard.

After the appearance of *Temora*, Macpherson went into decline. He received rather rough treatment, but managed to overcome this to become a British Governor overseas and then returned to reside in London. He produced a *History of Great Britain* and an English translation of the *Iliad*, which the critics inevitably panned. In 1780 he was returned as a Member of Parliament for Camelford, and again in 1784 and 1790. Eventually he retired to his native Badenoch, where he bought a small estate on which he built a large house designed by Adam, standing on the site of the ancient Castle of Raitt, near a stone circle, an appropriate juxtaposition of the present with the past, which was characteristic of his life. He died in 1796 with the wish that he be buried in Westminster Abbey, a wish duly fulfilled; he now rests in 'Poet's Corner'. But, whether he intended it or not, his work established the respect of scholars for the poems and stories of the old Gaelic order which existed in Ireland and then in Scotland over a thousand years previously. He did what other poets had done for repressed nationalities and minority linguistic communities, as, for example, the Finnish poet Elias Lonnrot: focus attention on the fact that a 'primitive' society as was thought to exist then in the Highlands of Scotland had in fact an honourable lineage and antecedents which could match the best and most civilized of societies in Macpherson's day. His reputation in Badenoch rests, not so much on his despoiled literary aspirations, but on his generosity to the poorer tenants of his Balavil estate which he acquired, and his selfless efforts to have the forfeited Cluny Macpherson lands restored to the family of Ewen Macpherson, attainted for his part in the Forty-five. The present Balavil house, between Kincraig and Kingussie, was burnt and partially rebuilt in 1903.

One era in the history of Strathspey is that associated with the Highland Clearances, a long enough process which culminated in the protection of the Highlander and his way of life in the Crofters Act of 1886. Though in the main the common folk of Strathspey escaped the horrors perpetrated by landowners in other parts of the Highlands (though there were notable exceptions, for instance, in Glen Banchor), there were conditions imposed on their life and living which caused no end of hardship and many people, unwilling to suffer oppression and uncertainty, simply opted for a life in the cities of Scotland, or else emigrated to Canada, the Americas and New Zealand. These conditions were often described by residents in the various Strathspey parishes or by outside observers; and they speak for themselves:

Abernethy and Kincardine (1796):

What they complain of chiefly is the method followed in letting their farms when their leases are expired. It is seldom that the tenants are called on to renew till within a few months of the term of removal, and then, perhaps, left for years in suspense before they are settled with, and tried for some addition every year, and every year receiving a summons of removal. The offers received are generally kept private; and when they get a lease, it is only for fifteen or nineteen years, which they think too short. The effects of this method are very bad, both for master and tenant: for during the last two or three years of the lease they are under apprehensions of being removed, and of course plough up what they ought, or would not, if they were certain of continuing, and all this while careless about the repairs of their houses and buildings. By these means they either hurt themselves, if they continue, or their successor if they remove, and the proprietor's interest in either case. Besides that, while people are kept long in suspense, it occasions much unhappy anxiety and restlessness of mind.

Kingussie (1796):

. . . To say the truth, the wretched appearance of numbers of them is sufficient proof of the hardships they endure. A few dividuals, perhaps, in the rank alluded to, may be found who are easy and affluent; but whoever is at pains to examine minutely the condition of the bulk of the people – to view the mean, ill-constructed huts in which they reside, – and to consider the scanty and precarious crops on which they depend in a great measure for subsistence, will be far from thinking that the picture of their misery is drawn in exaggerated colours.

## Duthil (1883):

. . . In addition to being compelled to yield up their right to their houses and offices, they were required during the currency of the lease – nineteen years – to reclaim so many acres of waste land, and bring it under cultivation. This, it is well known, could not be done under an outlay of from £20 to £24 an acre. The land so reclaimed is in its natural state only worth about 3d per acre yearly . . . after being reclaimed by the tenant, it is let by the proprietor at a yearly rent of 20s and sometimes more per acre. In this way the proprietor has hitherto been getting his waste lands improved, and his rental increased, by the sweat of the brow of the poor hard working tenant. In the district of Easter Duthil, for example, six or eight respectable families were removed from their comfortable homes to make room for a large sheep run where no such run should be . . . . It would be adding insult to injury to say that there were no removals from Strathspey for the last twenty years. I am assured on good authority that there were, and that some of them were of a painful and heartrending description . . . .

## Newtonmore (1846):

Newtonmore is smaller, in point of population, and much lower in point of comfort, than Kingussie. Here the propertyless, the dependent, and the wretched of the parish are gathered. Small pieces of land are attached to most of the houses; but few of them are larger than the ordinary village gardens; while the only external support given to the trade of the place is derived from a small number of crofters, who are located on a rocky acclivity that stretches back behind the hamlet. These crofters pay from £3 to £7 of rent, and are far from being comfortable in their circumstances – the nakedness of the soil giving the labour of the poor people no chance of adequate reward. It is a prevalent notion that it is small crofters, such as these, extracting a miserable crop of corn and barley from a few acres of barren land, that the clearance system removed from the glens. But the very opposite is the truth. The small tenants of this class are in fact creations of the clearance system. It would have been impossible to have found in the Highlands a collection of poverty like this Newtonmore, before that system was introduced. The small farmers who were cleared were greatly superior in their possessions and their condition to the crofters of the present day.

An indication of the removal of people from Strathspey is seen in population figures, such as that of Alvie which had 1092 recorded in 1831 and which was down to 564 in 1911; Abernethy: from 2092 in 1831 to 1228 in 1911; Laggan: down from 1196 to 754 in the same period. Of the clearance system Dr Samuel Johnson, who was not particularly noted for his love of the Scots or their traditions, found himself "full of the old Highland spirit, and was dissatisfied at hearing of rack rents and emigration. ... A rapacious chief would make a wilderness of his estate." An unprejudiced writer like Mrs Grant of Laggan bemoaned the rapacity of those who drove away the descendants of men whom their fathers led. Altogether, it was a sad period for many hundreds and thousands of common folk, wrenched by the force of political and economic circumstances, from the lands which their families had held, worked and used for their livelihood for generations. What was perhaps even sadder was the break up of the bond of trust and, often, friendship which had existed between those who lived on the land and those who, often by accident, sometimes by design, owned it. Inevitably, any such rupture leads to unhappiness; when it occurred in Highland society, albeit clan-based, it was a tragedy of the first order.

It has been said that the history of a people is reflected in its traditions, which show the true face of the contemporary members of the community. Of course, over the years traditions tend to be changed, often wrenched out of their original factual context, and, as often, fall out of belief as 'civilizing' influences make their impacts. However, one cannot live in an area without sensing, in one way or another, the redolent past, particularly when almost every square mile has an association with the past. Strathspey is thus no stranger to history and tradition, both of which span over 2000 years; and when tradition treads heavily around historical persons, it becomes that much more interesting.

What is supposed to be the first two-storey house to be built in Badenoch is the house of Ballachroan, between Newtonmore and Kingussie. It now stands empty and roofless and is accessible by way of a footpath off the A9 road for those who wish to taste the past. It has an eerie atmosphere, even in bright sunlight, which is perhaps not so surprising considering the man who built it in the late 1700s: Captain John Macpherson, An Offigear Dubh, the Black Officer. He was thought to have had a close association with the Devil. He was not a popular man in the district, mainly because of his energetic, sharp and often dishonest methods of raising recruits to fight in the French Wars. For one period of three years, the crops at Ballachroan surpassed any other that were grown in the district. People muttered that this could not have been achieved by natural means and concluded that only assistance from the Devil could have brought such results. But the Devil, they said, gives nothing for nothing; unless there is a return of some kind for his help he refuses to co-operate. So the locals worked the matter out with some sense of logic. In the first year of the supposed bargain between the Black Officer and the Devil, it was agreed that Ballachroan should have excellent crops, provided that the Devil had all that grew above ground. This the Black Officer agreed to, and promptly planted turnips, instead of oats and barley. At the end of the season all the Devil had for his bargain was a stack of shaws. In the second year the Devil insisted that he should have all that grew below ground. Again the Black Officer agreed and grew grain; the Devil's reward was stubble and roots. In the third year the Devil was more than anxious to ensure a profit from his bargain and demanded that all that could be enclosed within diagonal lines drawn from corner to corner across the fields. Again, the bold Captain agreed. But this time he planted nothing. And instead of keeping his cattle in the fields, he made circular enclosures of hurdles, which he moved from place to place as the grazing was used up. With no proper fields and with no corners to the temporary fields, no diagonals could be drawn, and the Devil had to admit defeat.

More than likely, the perfectly good explanation of the excellent products grown at Ballachroan was that the Black Officer was far ahead of his time in his farming methods. He was in fact the first man in that district ever to use a proper rotation of crops in his system of farming. One of the mechanical aids to farming which he used was a device like a capstan driven by horses. This was linked up with a winnowing-fan in the barn to winnow chaff and thus save a lot of human labour. But such was his reputation that the local ministers said that he was being blasphemous, for no one but God had the authority to raise winds.

There were other tales about the Black Officer, however, which defied explanation. The most notable concerned an event on the Monday preceding Christmas in the year 1799. Captain Macpherson and four other men went out deer hunting in the Forest of Gaick and made their base in a lodge there, a substantial stone-built structure which was occupied in the summer and autumn months by herdsmen and sportsmen. After a day out shooting, the men decided to make a good night of it, especially as the weather was threatening to break. And break it did. A storm of unparalleled fury broke. When Christmas had come and gone, and the men had not returned to Ballachroan, a man was sent to investigate the matter. This man, when he arrived at the place where he knew the lodge to have been, found absolutely nothing at first, not even the walls of the building. But after a little searching he came across a cap and a powder flask, which he recognized as belonging to one of the men in the Black Officer's hunting party. He returned to Kingussie with his tale and a search party made haste for Gaick where, after some hours of searching, they found the bruised and dead bodies of Macpherson and his friends. One corpse was found behind a dyke

Dailvane distillery and (*below*) the Aberlour-Glenlivet distillery.

Aberlour and (*below*) Craigellachie.

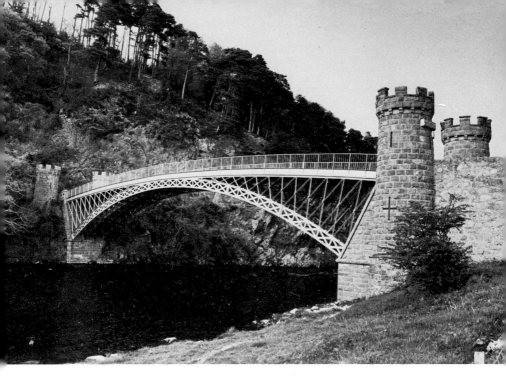

The old bridge at Craigellachie, designed and built by Thomas Telford in 1814 and (*below*) the new bridge which has largely replaced it.

Fochabers and (*below*) the old railway bridge which crosses the Spey to Garmouth.

Two views of the village of Kingston.

The Spey at Garmouth.

Garmouth.

Mending salmon nets at Spey Bay and (*below*) the currach used by
Alastair Mor, the legendary timber-floater.

some distance away from where the lodge had stood and where the other remains were found. What horrified the searchers most was that the gun-barrels of the hunters were bent and twisted and the wide-open staring eyes of the dead men had an indescribable look of horror in them. Local people said this was the outcome of the Black Officer's association with the Devil, who had in the end extracted his final demand of payment. Others said the deaths were due to something more sinister. Men who had previously been to the Gaick lodge with him claimed to have heard something heavy and soft, without bones, clumsily slithering about on the roof in its efforts to get inside. The destruction of the lodge and its inmates was more likely to have been the product of an avalanche of snow from an adjacent hillside. About 1922 an avalanche occurred at exactly the same spot which killed several hinds.

The Cat's Den is on Creagan a' Chait, on Kennapole Hill by Loch Gamhna. It is mostly associated with the legendary history of the Grants of Rothiemurchus; but its claim to fame rests on an incident nearer to our times and involves a character named Black Sandy Grant. During his younger years there were some on-goings at a place called the Croft, between Inverdruie and Loch an Eilean, wherein lived the young Laird of Grant. The source of the trouble was a young housekeeper in the employ of the Laird, who had already borne him three children. This fact was of no small concern to the old Laird who decided to call in Black Sandy to ask him how she could be stopped in her amorous activities. Sandy begged leave to solve the problem in his own way and, with the old Laird's consent, he felt to don a disguise, waylaid the unfortunate woman and cut off one of her ears. Of course, she was not able to identify her attacker, but Sandy thought it wise to move himself out of Rothiemurchus and live in Grantown, to concern himself with sheep-farming, satisfied that he had done a useful service for the old Laird of Grant. But not long afterwards he was involved in a fight with a cattle drover which ended in the drover being left for dead near Spey

Bridge. Now, Sandy found himself a marked man and, to escape the wrath and vengeance of the drover's friends, he emigrated to America. His obvious talents for enterprise found a place there and he became moderately prosperous. Fame was to come to his clan in the form of his son, Ulysses S. Grant, born in Ohio in 1822 and who became a President of the United States. The President visited his father's homeland before he died in 1885, and no doubt reflected on the quirks of fate which had brought him to that high position.

About a mile and a half east of Kingussie is an earth house, known as the Cave of Raitts. The word 'raitt' comes from a form of the Irish '*rath*', meaning a dwelling inside a hill, which was later to become associated with fairy knolls. It has been marked on maps as a 'Pictish House'. It forms a subterranean half-circle, narrow at the entrance but gradually widening to about eight feet across. The cave itself is about seventy feet long and about seven feet high. Tradition says that it was built by giants in prehistoric times. It was often used in more historic times, sometimes as a place of refuge and at other times as a habitation. One story connected with the cave tells of how the MacNiven of Dunachton, who once held the Barony of Dunachton, and his nine sons hid there until they were found and killed. The tradition is that Robert the Bruce gave the MacNiven lands to the Macphersons, who had been loyal to him in his campaigns for the Crown of Scotland. In retaliation, the MacNivens raided the Macphersons' cattle and carried them off. Rather than set the scene for a long feud, the Macphersons sent a daughter of the chief to parley with the MacNivens, with a view to reaching an amicable solution to the matter. But the poor girl was badly treated and sent home in humiliation. A party of Macphersons sallied forth to Dunachton to sort out the MacNivens, but found no trace of them; yet, for some months afterwards, it was obvious that they were still in the district. Meantime, a Macpherson adherent had become suspicious of a hut that had been erected at Raitts. To investigate the matter he disguised himself as a beggar to gain entry to the hut. In it he found two women who gave him some bread and told him to be off. But he insisted that he was ill and after some effective pleading was allowed to stay the night. Once inside the hut he saw the two women busily engaged in baking large quantities of scones which were placed in a cupboard. Yet the cupboard always seemed to be empty: the scones were feeding more mouths than had the two women. He reported back to the Macphersons and a party of armed men raided the hut, which they pulled down to discover the ill-fated MacNivens who were massacred to a man.

A number of fugitives from the aftermath of Culloden found safety and shelter in the cave during the Forty-five. Later the cave was occupied by a gang of robbers in 1773, which team of ruffians was broken up after their leader was hanged in Inverness.

All Highland districts had their witches, and Badenoch was no exception to the rule. Contemporary witches did much good in their communities, mainly the healing of minor ailments, sometimes by faith but more with the application of those herbal treatments which now, in our day, are being accepted as being as efficacious as many of the drugs prescribed by doctors. One witch however stands out in Badenoch legend, known as the Witch of Laggan, whose existence can be doubted. Inhabiting as she did the world of Highland folklore and legend, she contributed her portion to the tales told about her in the old *ceilidh* houses. Her end concerned a hunter, famed for his persecution of witches. One stormy night he was forced to take shelter from the bad weather in a lonely mountain bothy. While sitting in front of the fire a cat entered and disturbed his dogs so much that he had a difficult time trying to pacify them. At last the cat spoke and said: "I am a witch and have taken this shape. If you will shelter me I will give up my wicked ways."

The hunter took pity on her and invited her to sit by the fire. But this she refused to do until he had tied up his dogs and she offered him a rope with which to do this. He took the rope, and led the dogs to a corner of the bothy. But instead of tying the dogs, he tied the rope to a thick wooden beam. When the dogs had quietened down the cat changed its form and became the Witch of Laggan. Looking at the hunter she said, with sparking fires in her eyes, that as he had been a persecutor of her kind, the time had come for his own end. At this she flew at the hunter's throat, but not before the dogs leaped to the defence of their master. The witch, thinking that the dogs had not been tied securely shouted to the rope "Tighten, tighten". But all that happened was that the rope tightened its coils round the beam until it cracked. Realizing that she was not going to get the better of the situation, she fled out of the bothy, chased by the dogs who caught and snapped at her flying clothes. She eventually escaped and disappeared over the hills.

After the hunter returned home, his wife told him that there was news in the district: the Witch of Laggan was ill. He went to see her and when he uncovered the wounds on her face she shrieked and died. That same night two travellers met a blood-stained woman running in the direction of the churchyard with two black dogs chasing her. Next they met a black man on a black horse who asked them if they had seen a woman being chased by dogs. No sooner had they replied in the affirmative when the stranger turned his horse and made off in the direction of the churchyard to catch the witch just before she gained the sanctuary of the holy place. Later the travellers met the black man on his horse, with his dogs trailing behind, their great teeth sunk into the body of the witch who had finally met her end while trying to escape the clutches of her black master.

There are many old documents which mention the High-landers' love of dancing and the making of music. By the seventeenth century a rather characteristic form of music had made itself known and was singing its way into a popularity which still exists, to accompany the foursome reel, possibly the most popular Highland dance there is. The strathspey is the name given to tunes played in a comparatively slow tempo; they were called 'ports' and are found written down in the

Skene and Stralloch MSS (1615-1625 and 1627-29). They are ideally suited to the fiddle and a school of composers of tunes of this type developed in Strathspey. There is a tradition that the earliest of strathspeys was that played by James Macpherson who rendered his "Macpherson's Rant" at the foot of his gallows tree in 1700. The Cummings, who were hereditary fiddlers to the Lairds of Grant, were known to have had a hand in the development of this musical form. Between 1750 and 1830 the strathspey's popularity had reached its zenith and, indeed, so great was the demand for new tunes that many Strathspey fiddlers and composers moved to Edinburgh and to London to satisfy the demands of society for dancing to 'Scotch music', which was to develop the 'Scotch snap' – a short note (on the beat) followed by a long one occupying the rest of the beat. Some outstanding fiddlers now rest in the halls of fame, such as William Marshall (Fochabers) and Neil Gow (of Dunkeld) and his son Nathaniel Gow.

William Marshall was not only a composer of strathspey and reel tunes. He was born of humble but industrious parents. With the exception of some six months at a grammar school, he received no education but what his father had taught him. When he was twelve years of age he entered the service of the Duke of Gordon in Gordon Castle and remained there for thirty years to become factor to the Duke. He taught himself mechanics, astronomy, architecture and music. He was composing tunes long before he was persuaded to publish them. When eventually he did so, he found it necessary to state on the front cover of his book that the contents were all his own compositions and that other people had been changing the names of some of his tunes and publishing them as their own. This warning is supposed to have been directed chiefly at the Gows, for there are two footnotes to tunes in the book stating that the Gows had appropriated the melody and changed the name. Ethical standards were not particularly high in those days as regards copyright. Marshall composed some 114 strathspey tunes. The tune "Marquis of Huntly's Farewell" is regarded as the most beautiful strathspey ever composed, and one eminent musical authority asked "whether, with this tune, strathspey music has not said its vital last word". Marshall died in 1833 and is buried in Bellie church-yard, near Fochabers.

# VI

## EXPLOITATION

ONE OF the major and continuing assets of the Highlands is the forests. In the past, this was largely constituted in the Caledonian Forest, an extensive tract of woodland and scrub which, it is believed when man first entered Scotland, covered over half of the Scottish mainland area lying below 3000 feet. In time, the woods, seen as a source of fuel, building material and, later, charcoal, were depleted and only in the last century or so have attempts been made to replace the original land cover; even accepting that these attempts were made on a purely commercial basis and not with a view to replanting to restore the countryside.

That the Caledonian Forest was of significant economic importance to the Highland region is clear from many documentary references to the uses to which wood was put: from firewood to ship-building. Early man started the process of forest cutting which has lasted to modern times. Then, the extension of land cultivation encroached on more forest until it was realized by central authorities, the old Scots Parliament, that a serious problem was looming which would create a vacuum in the economy, if not in the lifetime of contemporary politicians, then at least in that of a future generation. So legislation was introduced by the middle of the fifteenth century to regulate the destruction of forests, though, in reality, it had little effect. Many woods were burnt to the ground to remove the natural cover of wolves, and also to imp out human predators: criminals and outlaws. Later, iron foundries were established which further depleted the forests,

By the end of the eighteenth century much of the original land cover as represented by the old Caledonian Forest had disappeared, particularly in the Cairngorms and in the valley of the Spey. Perhaps the last act of destruction was in the clearance of tree cover to provide sheep runs on a vast scale and which prevented natural regeneration. Although the pastures produced were fertile to begin with, they degenerated rapidly as the result of the natural cycle of chemical and organic activity associated with forest cover being broken. Subsequent loss by leaching became more pronounced, there being no forest litter to retain a proportion of the rainfall at the surface. Down-hill wash produced peat-forming processes. Bracken, once broken and bruised and kept in check by the hooves of grazing cattle, ran rife, because sheep and deer are selective grazers and avoid the spreading bracken-infested areas. One problem was compounded by another to produce the present sad picture of land degeneration in the Highlands. All these processes, however, produced an interesting panorama of economic exploitation which has added an extra dimension of interest to the history of the Spey valley.

When Edward Burt travelled in the Highlands in the 1720s, he was impressed by the number of uses of timber, as a replacement to iron which was then in short supply: "Almost all their implements for husbandry, which in other countries are made from iron, or partly of that metal, are in some parts of the Highlands entirely made of wood; such as the spade, plough-share, harrow, harness and bolts; and even locks for doors are made of wood." Other uses included timber for house-building, furnishing, carts and other vehicles, boats, domestic utensils, basket-work, ropes, with tree bark, particularly oak, being used for tanning and dyeing. The total use of tree produce, however, was not particularly extravagant and the forests were well able to recuperate from the demands made on them. A certain amount of economy in the use of timber was also practised, as seen in the old practice of removing the main roof timbers of a house if the occupant decided to remove to another part of the district; roof-timbers were in fact regarded as being the property of the tenant and an asset over which a landowner had no control. It was this fact which led to these timbers being burnt during the period of the Highland Clearances, to prevent the evicted occupants from erecting a house elsewhere. Deprived of this important asset, the evicted were truly homeless.

By the closing years of the seventeenth century, however, the light in which timber was regarded had changed from the domestic and incidental to a more commercial approach which introduced the new technique of forest management. Wood, particularly Scots pine, became a main attraction, along with the oak, the bark of which provided the main agent of the British tanning industry until the late nineteenth century. It was inevitable that commercial interests of a speculative nature would appear on the Highland timber scene; and this, indeed, did occur, particularly in the form of the York Buildings Company whose presence almost transformed the Spey valley from an area of local Highland interest to one of economic importance to the gross national product of Britain.

There were, however, historical factors which led to the introduction of this company to the Highlands. In the seventeenth century feuds between clans and their septs, and civil wars involving Scottish forces, reached a peak. Deeside, on the eastern side of the Cairngorms was an area for frequent battles and skirmishes. Added to that the fact that the folk in the Cairngorms area were partly Catholic and pro-Jacobite, and the stage was set for change of a painful nature. In the year 1688 the Whig General, Mackay, burned no less than twelve miles of very fertile Highland country, involving the destruction of up to 1400 houses in upper Deeside.

The rising of 1715 was an event which had a significance which stretched far into the future of the Highlands and was to create a series of circumstances in which outside factors and influences were able to take root to wrench the Highlands into a range of contemporary operations. It led to the rising three decades later which marked the end of a social order; frag-

mentation of the social structure and changes in land ownership produced profound changes, not in the least in the
attitudes of Highland landowners to the assets they possessed
in the form of land and timber, and increased their awareness
to exploit their holdings for profit. Those Highland chiefs who
had not become involved with the Jacobites in 1715 were able
to sit back and apply themselves to their enrichment. But for
those who had nailed their colours to the Jacobite mast, it was
a different tale. Their estates and titles became forfeit and
attainted, and their former lands came up for grabs to open up
the way of exploitation. Thus, the York Buildings Company
came on the Highland scene.

The company was established in 1691 by an Act of Parliament which enabled the company to raise the Thames water
in York Buildings in London and supply customers in St
James's and Piccadilly from its waterworks in the grounds of
York House. The company ended its life in 1818 with the
waterworks as its only asset, and that was worth a mere and
literal peppercorn. But the years between 1691 and 1818 were
to provide the company and its directors with many opportunities for speculation for profit. The improbable move from
supplying water to London's great aristocratic houses to an
involvement in agricultural and industrial operations in Scotland came about by the 1715 Rising. After the rising had been
reduced to simmering point, with an ineffective lid placed on
the efforts but not the aspirations of the Jacobites, a number of
Highland estates were forfeited under Acts of Attainder and
were put up for sale. An Act of Parliament of 1719 em-
powered the purchasers of forfeited lands to grant annuities on
the value of the estates, a corporate body being required to
exploit this opportunity. By a coincidence, the York Buildings
Company was offered for sale at the same time. A far-sighted
London solicitor saw the possibility of using the company as a
means of amassing great profit, and thus the company entered
the Highland scene as a landower, sometimes notorious and
unorthodox. It also brought to the Highlands Aaron Hill;
friend of the poets Savage and Thomson, he was himself a

dramatist and poet, traveller, manager of Drury Lane Theatre, a dabbler in political economy and an enterprising projector of schemes for profit.

The first whiff of speculation for the company arrived in the autumn of 1719 when the Government's Commissioners of Enquiry were ready to begin selling the estates of members of the Scottish aristocracy and land-owning class who had made errors of judgement in their support for the Jacobite cause. These lands were bought by representatives of the York Buildings Company, including the small estate of Rob Roy Macgregor at Inversnaid. The second whiff came in the person of Aaron Hill. He had behind him an impressive record of both success and failure; for instance, in the last year of Queen Anne's reign he had set up a Beech Oil Company, for making olive oil from the fruit of the beech tree, and the advantages of which he promoted in poetic verse:

> France shall no more her courted vineyards boast,
> But look with envy on our northern coast,
> Which now enriched with matchless oil and corn,
> Unequall'd vintages shall soon adorn.

Hill also became deeply involved in a plan to settle a new plantation in South Carolina, the money for which he tried to raise by setting up a lottery; this latter tack, however, was found to be illegal. But Hill was not without resource: if South Carolina was to prove a difficult venture, would not Scotland's woodlands provide a better area for speculation? In 1726 he visited Scotland and saw the great pine woods of Abernethy, on Speyside, which belonged to the Laird of Grant. The woods had been reported on for the Commissioners for the Navy in 1704 as "likliest to serve Her Majesty and Government" in terms of ship timber. Aaron Hill thought so too. On his return to London he persuaded the directors of the York Buildings Company to purchase the timber as it stood. The idea appealed to the company's principals and in January 1728 the company bought 60,000 trees of the best and finest of the fir woods on the Grant estate, at a price of

£7000. The wood was to be cut over a period of fifteen years. The company also took a lease for the same period of the Main and meadow of Coulnakyle, in the neighbourhood of the woods. Hill's report to the company was that the trees were fit to make main masts for the Navy's ships. However, when a specimen cargo was cut and sent to London, it was discovered that the trees were unsuitable for this purpose, though fit for secondary uses. The company, however, had made its agreement and possession of the woods had been taken meantime. There was, in any case, plenty of timber and it was hoped that enough would be obtained to make the whole speculative venture profitable. The cutting operations began on a large scale, with houses being built for the workforce, and mills and machinery erected. Many of the workmen were not paid in cash, but in promissory notes issued by William Stephens, an ex-Member of Parliament, ex-Governor of the State of Georgia, and who became supervisor of the company's operations on Speyside. Such was the esteem in which the company was held, and its credit and influence, that for a number of years these notes of hand circulated in the district and were accepted as reliable currency.

Aaron Hill put in an appearance at Abernethy, to survey the practical outcome of his schemes. He was received with great honours. The Duchess of Gordon extended her hospitality to him; the local gentry all pressed to make his acquaintance, and the Magistrates of both Inverness and Aberdeen presented him with the freedom of their burghs and entertained him with much respect. So carried away was he with the reception he got that he burst into a flowering of verse under the shadow of Cairngorm, amongst which was an address to his wife from "the Golden Groves of Abernethy". But effective public relations, as engineered by Hill, were no consolation to the real engineering problems which the company was experiencing with its timber operations.

Captain Edward Burt, who wrote when the operations were in full swing, doubted whether the company would ever

recover the costs of felling and removing trees from the area
"... over rocks, bogs, precipices, and conveyance by rocky
rivers, except such as are near the sea coast, and hardly those,
as I believe the York Buildings Company will find in the
conclusion". This was a piece of intelligent predicting, for in
the course of four years the charge on the timber trade had
exceeded its returns by nearly £28,000. Another observer was
the Reverend John Grant, the parish minister, who noted:

> ... the most profuse and profligate set that were ever heard of in
> this corner. ... This was said to be a stock-jobbing business.
> Their extravagancies of every kind ruined themselves and
> corrupted others. Their beginning was great indeed, with 120
> working horses, waggons, elegant temporary wooden houses,
> saw-mills, iron-mills, and every kind of implement and appa-
> ratus of the best and most expensive sorts. They used to display
> their vanity by bonfires, tar barrels, and opening hogsheads of
> brandy to the country people, by which five of them died in one
> night. They had a commisary for provisions and forage at a
> handsome salary, and in the end went off in debt to the pro-
> prietors and the country. But yet their coming to the country
> was beneficial in many respects, for besides the knowledge and
> skill which was acquired from them, they made many useful and
> lasting improvements. They made roads through the woods.
> They erected proper saw-mills. They invented the construction
> of the raft as it is at present, and cut a passage through a rock in
> Spey, without which floating to any extent could never be
> attempted.

This minister, however much he expressed disapproval of
the company's influences on his flock, was not behind the door
when it came to making the proverbial fast buck. When the
workmen of the company were paid in gold, they went to the
Rev. Grant for change, which he provided at a rate of twenty
shillings to the guinea.

To diversify its operations, the company set up iron furnaces in the neighbourhood where 'Glengarry' and 'Strath-
down' iron pigs were produced, with another four furnaces set
up to make bar iron. For these furnaces great quantities of

wood were cut down in the Abernethy area. The amount of charcoal produced exceeded the requirements of the iron-making operations and large shipments of the material were made to England and Holland. The iron venture was, however, no more profitable than the timber operation and large debts began to accrue against this side of the company's interests.

On the company's other business fronts, too, problems appeared daily and began to pile up into a huge legal mess which took until 1818 to sort out, when the company's only asset was the original waterworks in London. Even that was being challenged by the New Chelsea Water Works, in the favour of which the York Buildings Company gave an under-taking not to engage to supply water, as a public water company, for a period of 2000 years, and demised the fee simple of their property, from September 1818, at a yearly rental of a peppercorn.

Some 150 years of operation by the company were reduced to nothing by inexpertise. Even though the conduct of the company's business showed considerable ingenuity, most of its schemes were wanting in honesty. It became over-burdened with capital speculations and failed to operate its various trading ventures with a view to profit. Decades of litigation cost a fortune; the litigations in the Court of Sessions in Edinburgh alone are said to have cost the company £3000 a year. Indeed, many of the decisions in these litigations have now become leading cases and it is said, too, that contemporary questions in every department of company law have at one time been settled in the past at the expense of the York Buildings Company. Though it ceased to exist as a business venture in 1818, a century later it was reported that money lay in Scottish banks which represented the unclaimed dividends issued by the company in its lifetime. Certainly, if Scotland as a whole did not reap much benefit from the company's sojourn in the country, Scots lawyers gained a worthwhile living from it.

It was undoubtedly the proximity of the River Spey and its

tributaries to the Forest of Abernethy which gave Aaron Hill the idea of exploiting the timber of the forest and exporting it out of the area by a water route. Otherwise, the venture would have had nothing to offer the York Buildings Company, for it would have had to lay down an infrastructure of communications as a pioneering exercise, to put roads where there were none before. However, the Spey had a long association of use as a means to convey timber from the forests along its banks to its mouth. Before the company came along, the owners of the woodlands in the Spey valley had been accustomed to floating their timber down the river; the logs were either single or in lots, loosely tied together and attended by men working from a currach, "a small basket of wickerwork covered on the outside with an ox-hide". Rafting timber had not been thought of until Aaron Hill arrived on the scene and introduced the method without delay. Large trees, with deals and boards, were bound together. On the top were placed benches for the floaters, who, armed with oars, conducted the rafts down the Spey to its mouth at Garmouth. The country people soon learned to take advantage of this new means of transport and floated down on their own rafts with the produce of butter, cheese, skins, bark and lime. Indeed, rafting on Highland rivers became something of a boon to new industries in the region and it was not long after Hill's introduction of rafting on the Spey that other Highland rivers carried on their waters massive quantities of cut timber to saw-millers and charcoal burners. But before rafting could become commonplace, the Spey had to be tamed for taking the rafts, and the rafters, or floaters, trained from sailing their small light currachs or coracles to navigate large masses of timbers through the waters of the river.

The currach was widely used in the Spey valley as a means of transport. It was a flat-bottomed, slightly oval and almost tub-like affair, constructed with a frame of wickerwork over which was fitted the skin of a horse, cow or deer. The craft was fitted with a seat and equipped with a wooden paddle, which looked something like a garden spade. The craft could be carried on a man's back, often for miles, to get to the waters of a Spey tributary. One man achieved some degree of fame for his stamina. Known as Alastair Mor na Curach, Alastair of the Coracle, he was a member of a group of families with a long association of timber floating to Spey- mouth. The currach-men were on the scene when the York Buildings Company arrived, and it was they, more than likely, who added an incentive to Aaron Hill to form a scheme to exploit the Abernethy woods. A description of these currach- men dates from 1859:

> Two families of Grant, named Mor (bog) and Odhar (pale or of yellow complexion), who lived at Tulchan, on the Spey, were the first who ventured on this perilous voyage. The first raft consisted of eight trees, fastened together by a hair rope. One or two men went into the Curach to guide the raft, others from the shore, with ropes fastened to the tail end of the raft, acted as a rudder. On the second trip a dozen trees were brought down. The Curach was always carried back from the mouth of the Spey on the back of a stalwart Highlander, who had obtained the name of Alister Mor na Curach. This worthy occupied the farm of Dalcroy, on the Spey, and lived to the age of 106 years.

It is thought that the Strathspey currach now preserved in Elgin Museum, the last of its kind in Scotland, is the one used by Alastair Mor during the period of the timber-floating activities of the York Buildings Company. If this is so, it is interesting to reflect that such an ancient mode of water transport, primitive yet effective, and surviving into the early eighteenth century, came into its own in a final burst of economic importance during the semi-industrialized activities of a London share-speculation Company after 1728.

Some of the first documentary mentions of the currach being used on the River Spey date back to the late fifteenth century, when the craft was used in connection with catching salmon with nets, and presumably used to take the men out to the nets to remove the fish. The value of these craft is seen in the prices paid for hides: 8s; in 1510, a hide was purchased "for a currock" for 10s 4d, while another hide was "barked and fitted" for 2s. Most of the documentary references indicate that the currach was used in conjunction with nets for fishing salmon in rivers and lochs; the currach-men seem to have been employees of the local estate rather than fishers on their own account. By the opening years of the eighteenth century, the currach was being used to guide logs or sawn deals down the Spey and its main tributary rivers.

When the York Buildings Company bought its trees from the Laird of Grant in 1728, it also purchased the use of existing sawmills on the River Nethy. In the early days of its operations, the company had some 18 currachs employed in floating small rafts of sawn deals. Progress was slow, however, until Aaron Hill suggested that larger quantities of timber could be floated with an advantage to the company's profits.

Hill evolved a method of constructing a large raft "consisting of two or three branders (crossbars) of spars in the bottom joined end to end, with iron or other loups, and a rope through them, and conducted by two men, one at each end, who have each a seat and oar, with which they help the raft in the proper direction". Each of these larger rafts could carry up to £20-worth of timber at an average cost per raft per journey of £1 10s. The Spey had, however, to be made navigable by the removal of large rocks in the river. This was done by a method produced by Hill's fertile brain. When the water in the river was low, men made "large fires on the rocks when the stream was low, and then throwing water on the heated surface. The stone was thus calcined or fractured and rendered easy of removal."

The timber activities started by the York Buildings Company in Abernethy continued for many decades, there being a constant demand for wood for many purposes, but particularly for the needs of war. Britain was always in a state of perpetual warfare with one Continental power or another, France, Spain, and Holland, and there was a basic need for timber. Due to the shrinking sources of the supply of timber in England, and the hazards attending the bringing of supplies from Scandinavia and far-off New Brunswick (especially in time of war), it fell on the woods of Speyside to keep up with the demand. In 1784 another company bought the forest timber of Glenmore from the Duke of Gordon and the rafting industry on the Spey was resuscitated, bringing considerable trade to both Upper Speyside and to the villages at the mouth of the river: Garmouth and Kingston. In addition, the increased activity had not escaped the notice of other landowners in Speyside, and they, too, began to exploit their wealth in timber. The Glenmore Forest was perhaps the most important and extensive operation. In 1794 it was reported that:

> The quantity of spars, deals, logs, masts and ship-timber, which they send to Garmouth or Speymouth yearly, is immense and every stage of the process of manufactory, brings money to the country; generally once a year they send down Spey a loose float, as they call it, of about 12,000 pieces of timber of various kinds, whence they send it to England, or sell it round the coast. For some years, they have sent great numbers of small masts or yards to England to the King's yards, and other places, and have built about 20 vessels of various burdens at Garmouth or Speymouth, all of Glenmore fir ... The fir-woods of this country exceed all the natural fir-woods in Scotland put together, without comparison. Sir James Grant's woods of Abernethy, of many miles in circumference; next, the Duke of Gordon's in Glenmore; then Mr Grant of Rothiemuchus's, who is supposed to have more trees than either of them; then the Duke's again; after that the Laird of McIntosh's in Glenfishy, all in a line, of about 20 miles in length, on the south side of the Spey. ... Besides Sir James Grant has another wood, of an excellent quality ... on the River Dulnain.

Other documentary sources indicate that these "loose floats", as distinct from the rafts, could number up to 20,000 logs and spars and were accompanied by up to eighty men who went along the riversides with long poles, pushing off the timber when it stuck. The men got 1s 6d a day, with free whisky rations. Rafts were still used, but only for sawn timber, and consisted of about fifty spars bound together, on which deals and other sawn timber were laid. The rafters or floaters who saw these rafts safely down the Spey to Garmouth, then returned home carrying on their shoulders the iron hooks and ropes used in making up the rafts.

The life of the floaters, while it carried a sense of romance, was hard and often dangerous. The life and work of the floaters is vividly described by Elizabeth Grant of Rothiemurchus in her *Memoirs of a Highland Lady*:

> The logs prepared by the loppers had to be drawn by horses to the nearest running water, and there left in large quantities till the proper time for sending them down the streams. It was a busy scene all through the forest, so many rough little horses moving about in every direction, each dragging its load, attended by an active boy as guide and remover of obstructions. . . . This driving lasted till sufficient timber was collected to render the opening of the sluices profitable. . . .In order to have a run of water at command, the sources of the little rivers were managed artificially to suit floating purposes. Embankments were raised at the ends of the lakes in the far-away glens, at the point where the different burnies issued from them. Strong sluice-gates, always kept closed, prevented the escape of any but a small rill of water, so that when a rush was wanted the supply was sure.
>
> The night before a run, the man in charge of that particular sluice set off up the hill, and reaching the spot long before daylight opened the heavy gates; out rushed the torrent, travelling so quickly as to reach the deposit of timber in time for the meeting of the woodmen. . . . The duty of some was to roll the logs into the water; this was effected by the help of levers. . . . The next party shoved them off with long poles into the current, dashing in often up to the middle of the water when any case of obstruction occurred. They were then taken in charge by the most picturesque group of all, each supplied with a clip, a very long thin pole and flexible at one end, generally a young tall tree; a sharp hook was fixed to the bending point, and with this, skipping from rock to stump, over brooks and through briers, this agile band followed the log-laden current, ready to pounce on any stray lumbering victim that was in any manner checked in its progress. There was something graceful in the action of throwing forth the stout yet yielding clip, an exciting satisfaction

as the sharp hook fixed the obstreperous log. The many light forms springing about among the trees, along the banks that were sometimes high, and always rocky, the shouts, the laughter, the Gaelic exclamations, and above all, the roar of the water, made the whole scene one of the most inspiriting that either actors or spectators could be engaged in.

One or two of these streams carried the wood straight to the Spey, others were checked in their progress by a loch; when this was the case, light rafts had to be constructed, and paddled or speared over by a man standing on each raft. The loch crossed, the raft was taken to pieces, some of the logs left at a saw-mill, the rest sent down the recovered stream to the Spey; there the Spey floaters took charge of them. . . .

The Spey floaters lived mostly down near Ballindalloch, a certain number of families by whom the calling had been followed for ages, to whom the wild river, all its holes and shoals and rocks and shiftings, were as well known as had its bed been dry. They came up in the season, at the first hint of a spate, as a rise in the water was called. A large bothy was built for them at the mouth of the Druie in a fashion that suited themselves; a fire on a stone hearth in the middle of the floor, a hole in the very centre of the roof just over it where some of the smoke got out, heather spread on the ground, no window, and there, after their hard day's work, they lay down for the night, in their wet clothes – for they had been perhaps hours in the river – each man's feet to the fire, each man's plaid round his chest, a circle of wearied bodies half stupefied by whisky, enveloped in a cloud of steam and smoke, and sleeping soundly till the morning . . . the Ballindalloch men seized the logs, which were bored at each end by an auger, two deep holes into which iron plugs were hammered, the plugs having eyes through which well-twisted wattles were passed, thus binding any given number together. When a raft of proper size was thus formed it lay by the bank of the river awaiting its covering; this was produced from the logs left at the saw-mills, generally in the water, in a pool formed to hold them. As they were required by the workmen, they were brought close by means of the clip, and then by the help of levers rolled up an inclined plane and on to the platform under the saw; two hooks attached to cables kept the log in its place, the sluice was then opened, down poured the water, the great wheel turned, the platform moved slowly with the log, the saw-frame worked up and down, every cut slicing deeper until the whole length fell off. The squared logs were then cut up regularly into deals and carted off to the rafts where they were laid as a sort of flooring. Two rude gears for the oars completed the appointments of a Spey float. The men had a wet berth of it, the water shipping in, or, more properly, over, at every lurch; yet they liked the life, and it paid them well. Then they had idle times great part of the year, could live at home and till their little crofts in their own lazy way, the rent being made up by the floating.

Rafting on the Spey was not without its hazards. Often rafts would be swept out to sea at the mouth of the river, across the bar of sand and shingle and its crew never seen again, particularly if the incident occurred in the dense sea mists that frequently occur along the coast of the Moray Firth. Men were also lost by accidents in felling and, in particular, by being crushed by heavy logs in the rivers.

Apart from timber-felling for ship-building and other purposes, the valuable iron deposits in the Tomintoul district made considerable inroads into the Abernethy woods. The York Buildings Company erected smelting works near Nethy Bridge and the wood from the adjacent forests used to produce charcoal. Innumerable horses were used to carry the basic iron ore in panniers over the hills for the distance of fifteen miles which separated the mines from Nethy Bridge. The ore mined contained a certain percentage of manganese, which was separated and taken, again by hill ponies, to Garmouth for shipment to the south. This enterprise of the company, as did the timber operation, failed to produce a profit and eventually only traces of the iron works remained in the neighbourhood of Abernethy.

The proximity of so much timber to the mouth of the Spey made it almost inevitable that ship-building would become established as an industry, and it fell to the small coastal settlement of Kingston to fill the role. Originally known as the Port of Garmouth, the larger and older village lying less than a mile from it to the east, it received its *anglice* name at the end of the eighteenth century. Its economic importance began when two Yorkshire timber merchants set up business in the village; they were known as raff merchants who specialized in importing timber in sawn deals. Their keen Yorkshire minds obviously saw the advantage in exporting their timber in the form of ships, using some of these, as they did, to carry timber to the markets in the south. Though no trace now exists of the former shipyard, it was an extremely busy place, with the ships being launched into the sea and then warped inside the mouth of the river for outfitting and completion. The Yorkshire influence, derived from one of the merchants coming from Kingston-on-Hull, was placed on the old Port of Garmouth, and the new settlement thus became a child of an English city.

The history of the Kingston shipbuilding industry started in 1786 when these two Yorkshire men, Mr Osbourne and Mr Dodsworth, set up their shipyard. During the first decade, about twenty-five vessels were built and then a further thirty ships until the yard closed down in 1815. That the firm gave up building ships in the same year as Waterloo is probably a pointer to the reason for the closure, since that historic event rang down the curtain on the immensely costly and ruinous Napoleonic Wars and introduced a period of financial exhaustion and a severe slump in trade. The closure then, as it does nowadays, threw many men out of work and Kingston became a backwater. A number of skilled shipwrights emigrated to the Miramichi district of New Brunswick to take up work with a William Davidson from Inverness, who needed ships to export the commercial salmon fishing produce to the Mediterranean and other ports in Europe. The connection between Kingston and Miramichi was further strengthened by a quirk of fate.

On a voyage from New Brunswick to Sunderland, with a cargo of timber, the brig *Adventurer* was totally wrecked on the treacherous sand and shingle bar at the mouth of the Spey when running for shelter in a storm. The crew were saved by the efforts of a young man, Alexander Geddie, whose father, a shipwright, was on the point of emigrating to New Brunswick. Geddie *père* decided to gamble on buying the wreck of the *Adventurer*, and he succeeded in refloating it by means of herring barrels tied to the stricken ship. Making use of the facilities in the deserted shipyard at Kingston, he restored the ship to seaworthiness and sold it at a handsome profit, the proceeds of which he used to build a new shipyard which was to last for three-quarters of a century.

Where canny Yorkshiremen had pulled out in the face of a national depression in the industry, the local man set his face against the odds and succeeded. Some 350 ships were to be built at Kingston yard, exclusive of fishing craft. After the Geddie yard was closed down the family emigrated to Natal. Many years later an old chest was discovered in which there were many constructional details of some of the ships built at Kingston; the find was valuable from the point of view that many ships in those days were constructed by rule of thumb methods and the shipwrights relied little on draughtsmanship. These documents now rest in the Science Museum, South Kensington, London, and fill a gap in the records of ships of the time.

Also closely associated with the Geddies in ship-building at Kingston were the Kinlock family, who thrived with the Geddies in their trade in an age when most of the world trade was moving from small ports or open beaches by comparatively small ships. Not only did Strathspey provide timber but the countryside was not disturbed by internal strife or wars which periodically put their Continental rivals out of business. These were the days when Britain truly ruled the waves and any ship flying the red duster received preferential treatment in most foreign ports. The Kinlocks celebrated this prosperity by naming one of their ships *Britannia*.

In all, the Kinlocks built over fifty ships and most of these were 99-ton schooners. The Kinlocks launched two vessels a year and in their best twelve months launched 1400 tons of shipping. Many of these were built for local owners and engaged in world trade. The largest vessel was the 800-ton barque *Lord Macduff.* Owned by Captain MacDonald of Garmouth and engaged in the china trade, she was referred to as the *Mighty Macduff* in the Moray Firth waters.

The Kinlocks began to retain the ships they built and called them the Chief Line, although they were more widely known in shipping circles as the Lockie Chiefs. There was the barque *Ocean Chief,* the barquentines *Scottish Chief, Wandering Chief, Leading Chief, Indian Chief, Kaffir Chief, Afghan Chief,* and finally the *Moray Chief,* built in 1888. These were kept in the Cape, and East and West India trade routes. Then in the early 1880s the fortunes of Speymouth began to change: steam began to replace sail and the River Clyde took the lead by building in steel. Worse still, the forests inland were becoming exhausted and timber was having to be brought from the Baltic and North America. Finally, the River Spey changed its course, leaving Garmouth an inland port with water not deep enough for launching.

It was the discovery by Henry Bessemer of the open-hearth process in the manufacture of steel which reduced the production cost of steel from £50 to £10 a ton, and which brought the Kingston yard to a halt, to close it for all time. Liners began to be built on the Clyde, made of iron, and the demand for wooden ships ceased.

The ships built at Kingston included barques, barquentines and schooners (the two former ships having each three masts (fore, main and mizzen, and the latter generally having a fore and main mast only). The ships were mostly merchant traders, the smaller ones engaging in the coastal and Baltic trades, while the larger served in the Cape, South American, Australian and China routes. Some were later to sail as whalers and sealers in the Greenland and David Straits. One ship was specially built for one or other of the expeditions which went in search of the Sir John Franklin expedition to the Arctic. Another ship, the *Chieftain,* of 600 tons, was destined to make her name as a China tea-clipper and was considered to have had a sporting chance of winning the 1858 homeward race from Hong Kong with the first cargo of that season's tea. While she did not win that celebrated race, she did reach London in less than the magic 100 days.

One Kingston-built ship was the subject of a sea mystery. She was the *Satellite*, a barquentine of 300 tons built by the Geddie yard in 1867. She sailed for Valparaiso in 1869 and was not heard of for some months. At first it was thought she had gone down in a storm with all hands until she was seen in a South American port and then in Rio de Janeiro. An attempt was made to catch up with the ship which was eventually traced, with her master, at Baltimore, where the captain was arrested for pirating. Unfortunately at that time there was a lack of documentary evidence and the necessary witnesses, and the master escaped scot free to disappear from human ken. In those days it was possible for a ship's master to have full control of the chartering of his owner's vessel, and to handle cash payments for freights; thus, many a sea captain retired early on the proceeds of illegal transactions.

From the exploitation of the woodland resources of the Spey valley in the eighteenth century to the exploitation of its scenic resources in the mid-nineteenth and twentieth centuries is but a step in the same direction; the latter, in terms of the preservation of fragile areas, is causing as much concern from conservationists as are those worried about the sociological implications of an area subjected to intense developmental pressures as the need increases for 'wilderness areas' to be offered to those whose normal and everyday environments fail to offer relaxation and leisure pursuits.

An indication of the pressures being created by the tread of many feet in the Grampians was suggested in a survey published in 1970, which showed that the damage which people have caused has reduced the covering of vegetation considerably, and in some areas has actually led to soil erosion. Particularly on the high ground in the mountain slopes, chemical weathering is very weak; this fact, coupled with the other factor of little available organic matter from decomposing plants being able to accumulate in what sparse soil covering there is, produces a serious problem. Mountain soils, in particular, are at great risk, as are the plant communities which rely on them for their continuity. Damage is most apparent on the soils and vegetation near ski-lifts. Added to this is the scarring of areas for tourist development, the pollution of certain lochs and streams and the unthoughtful scattering of litter of the kind that cannot be broken down by normal weathering processes, and there is created the present concern which, fortunately, is being joined by those very tourists who visit the Cairngorms and learn something of the delicate balances which exist in the Cairngorms, and have their respect for the countryside enhanced as a result. Many tourists are converted to active conservationists.

The most acute problems created by tourism in the Cairngorms area are quite serious. Cairngorm itself has been sacrificed to tourism while Braeriach, a National Nature Reserve, remains undeveloped. The Cairngorm development was, however, a natural if not reasonable development, since tourism in the form of hill-walking and mountaineering had been developed over many years at Glen More Lodge on the lower slopes of the mountain, though catering for numbers which were small in comparison with the present influx of people. In addition, in the context of offering sophisticated ski-ing facilities, the summit plateau of Cairngorm being around 4000 feet, snow tends to lie late in spring and allows ski-ing for much of the winter. In 1967 a number of the then local authorities, whose boundaries included parts of the Cairngorm area, produced a report indicating the desirable form which tourist development should take. But the report was produced after much of the existing development had taken place, and the restraints which were then thought desirable were used as alleviating factors for future developments. The report was useful in that it not only viewed development of the area in the economic and material sense, but also in considering how such intangibles as 'wilderness value' might be preserved before it disappeared as a commodity.

Problems still exist, however. Speculators wish to build new roads and hotels, and there have even been proposals to build whole villages high up the mountainsides; these activities, if left uncontrolled, will endanger many of the present attractions of the Spey valley, either directly by disturbance or indirectly by damaging or destroying the habitats of existing flora and fauna. There is yet to be produced a rational plan to describe, assess and evaluate the resources of fragile areas, and to decide which of these areas must remain inviolate wilderness and reserves for wildlife, and which areas can absorb development and change.

One of the problems hinted at already is the lack of information about how people and machines affect the stability of the countryside. An example of how land can be scarified was once seen around the White Lady complex of ski lifts and tows, where land vegetation was completely denuded over an area of about 800 acres. This came about originally by the use of bulldozers to erect the ski-lifts (bulldozers are also used to push snow onto the ski-runs when winds have blown them bare). Access roads for these machines were driven straight up the hillside, forming giant drains and which were against all the rules of ploughing on steep slopes. Similar channels have been bulldozed up the ski-tows to collect snow. The main factor here is economic. To pay their way the ski-lifts must be kept running in summer and many tourists take the opportunity to go up in the lifts and walk down. In some places the vegetation hereabouts is dominated by the moss *Rhacomitrium lanuginosum*, which is very easily destroyed by trampling on it. The 'drains' thus formed have created their own problems. The resultant erosion in 1968 actually undermined one of the pylons of the chair lift and some danger still exists from a quick snap thaw or a summer cloud burst. When these developments were being provided, ecologists were not consulted as to how damage could be minimized. As it is at the moment, the cost of change is too prohibitive and all that can be done is to monitor damage and control its effects.

The feasibility of the tourist complex at Aviemore, more than a decade after it was created, is still a matter of some argument, in the context of the massive all-year-round influx of tourists and the impact this has had on communities in the Spey valley. While the development has undoubtedly provided a much-needed shift of gravity from the south of Scotland into the Highlands, and provided both full- and part-time employment, it has been a matter of continuing debate whether the Spey valley communities have really gained so much. The dominant emphasis on tourism in the area has changed certain essential characteristics of some affected communities and has weakened the social fabric of the indigenous life which existed before 1965 when the speculators moved in.

Perhaps it can be said that the Spey valley tourist industry began when the old Highland estates were broken up, with their conversion into sporting areas, a development which led to depopulation and inferior forms of land use. Of course, then it was only the rich who could afford either to buy or rent land for their enjoyment and it was to these the landowners looked to supplement their incomes. The emergence of old clan and family lands as sporting estates began towards the end of the eighteenth century.

One of the first, if not the first, to recognize the possibilities for sport, with gun and rod, of the Highland estates was the indomitable Colonel Thomas Thornton, an eccentric sporting Yorkshire squire who pioneered the English sport invasion in the Highlands. In 1804 he wrote a big book *Sporting Tour in the Northern Part of England and Great Part of the Highlands of Scotland*, based on his visit to the Highlands some twenty years previously. Around 1783 he was in the Badenoch area on a reconnoitring visit "living during the time he was there in tents". This tour was in the nature of a preparation for his big tour which was conducted in 1786 in a grand style. Some idea of the extent of his baggage may be had from the fact that he hired a cutter, the *Falcon*, to take his creature comforts from Hull to Fochabers; so extensive were his requirements that it needed forty-nine carts to take it all from Fochabers to Badenòch, while four more horses were employed to transport on a sledge two large boats for his own use on the lochs. To the natives of Strathspey, the colonel's cavalcade must have seemed ominous, as the invading army wound its way around the hills.

He first resided at Raitts, two miles north of Kingussie, in rented accommodation, from which base he made many excursions into the immediate areas. He was one of the first contributors to depopulation. In 1789, the factor to the Duke of Gordon wrote to his master: "As Colonel Thornton now insists on having full possession, I have been obliged to bring a removal against the subtenants at Linwailg [now Linwilg] in order to make room for him . . . I would try settling with the subtenants for the remainder of the farm and reserve a few acres for the Colonel at the east end of Loch Alvie, which was the spot he seemed fondest of."

The Colonel recorded some of his 'bags'. In Dulnain at Carr-bridge: ". . . the game on these moors is innumerable. In a mile long, and not one half broad, I saw at least 1000 brace of birds" (red grouse). He recorded a fantastic gamebag of 561 birds and mammals of fifteen species, and 1126 fish.

The colonel's exploits and the size of his gamebags brought to the notice of others and they followed him into Badenoch. Invertromie was reported to be abounding "with hill and dale and well stocked with game, and allowed by most people to be an excellent quarter for a sportsman", the latter being Colonel Gordon, styled as Glentromie, who once "brought his brood of five sons up to Glentromie in a boat set on wheels, which, after performing coach on the roads, was used for loch fishing in the hills".

The takeover of land in the Spey valley continued with the displacement of the local population by those who could afford to buy or lease estates. Writing in 1848, one Robert Somers stuck to his criticism of the landlords and the large tenant farmers he met, the latter of whom he described as having been "raised to a position of wealth and indolence over the necks of the people". He wrote that their elevation had been a direct cause of pauperism and that they grudged paying even a trifling poor rate. He describes his visit to Badenoch:

> In Badenoch a great proportion of the farms are occupied by gentlemen who were at one time connected with the army. A stranger is amazed at the majors, and captains, and lieutenants, with whom he finds a peaceable country so thickly planted; and as they are all Macphersons or Macintoshes, he is apt to get completely bewildered in attempting to preserve their respective identities. These gentlemen are officers who received their commissions from the Duchess of Gordon, and who, on returning home from the wars, founded upon their services in the field a claim to a comfortable agricultural settlement. Their demand was allowed, but these military farmers, generally speaking, have not been successful . . . To make room for these gentlemen of the army, the small farmers were pushed to the wall. While the village of Kingussie was in a growing state, it offered asylum to the people thus cleared from the land; and when its population began to run over, a smaller village, called Newtonmore, received its refuse. In these two villages, and in a few small crofts scattered over the barren spots of the parish, have been deposited the dregs of wretchedness, which here, as elsewhere, have been produced by extensive clearances.

The real opening up of the Highlands as a tourist attraction came with Sir Walter Scott's writings; his letters, narrative poems and novels described an attractive alternative to the 'Grand Tour of Europe', which until the 1830s, had been a 'must for those who wished to finish and polish their education'. Another shot in the arm was given by Queen Victoria with her tour and the purchase of Highland estates in the Deeside Highlands. Grouse shooting had begun to be fashionable in the 1820s; by 1850 the letting of grouse moors was common practice. The end of the beginning came when the steam train puffed its way north to create accommodation centres such as Boat of Garten and Aviemore in the 1860s. Indeed, it was the advent of the Highland Railway which created the basis of the village of Aviemore as it is now known. The original settlement there provided no fewer than

140 employees for much-needed work on the railway.

Though the Highlands caught the tail-end of the railway fever which swept through Britain in the early days of the commercial iron road, the fever was no less intense and, as such fevers do, produced many schemes put forward by rival factions. Part of the reason for the Inverness–Perth rail route being opened was based on the need to transport timber from the Strathspey woodlands. By the mid-nineteenth century, neither the old method of floating logs down the Spey, nor the road transport available, was entirely satisfactory for large amounts. So it was not surprising that two prominent land-owners, the Earl of Seafield and Thomas Bruce, became leaders in the promotion of the Inverness and Perth Junction Railway, which was to find itself constantly in conflict with the Great North of Scotland Railway which offered to take passengers from Inverness to the south via Aberdeen, a long and tedious journey. In 1860 the directors of the Inverness and Perth Junction Railway decided to revive an unsuccessful rail scheme from 1845, with the engineer in both schemes being Joseph Mitchell, a brilliant engineer with a long record to his credit for roads, bridges and harbours schemes in the Highlands.

The scheme as redrawn in 1860 had the route passing through Boat of Garten and Grantown, instead of Carr-bridge. One reason for this was that both Seafield and Bruce wished the railway to pass close to their estates. Indeed, had this not been done to consolidate their support, the railway would not have been built. The route was constructed at a cost of £900,000 and the Aviemore–Boat of Garten–Forres section of the line was opened in 3rd August 1863, the route being completed when the Pitlochry–Aviemore section was opened a month later. The direct line from Aviemore to Inverness was opened in November 1898 as the result of fierce disputes between the Highland Railway Company and the Great North of Scotland Railway.

While the new routes carried a certain amount of freight in the form of timber and livestock, passenger traffic grew slowly and along with it the tourist trade. The railway made it possible for large numbers of people to get north into areas which previously had been as remote to them as were parts of Central Africa, if only to confirm what Sir Walter Scott had written about the Highlands, and possibly to tread the Highland ways and byways which had carried Queen Victoria in her tours. At first the summer visitors were from the wealthier classes who came for shooting and fishing safaris, sometimes in the special carriages they hired for their large parties; afterwards tourism became more broadly based and by the 1900s, the railway was catering for a wide range of people in their excursions to Inverness and farther north. Summer traffic tended to reach its peak just before the start of the grouse season on 12th August. Communities in the Spey valley, which had hitherto been isolated and circumscribed, began to cater for the incoming visitors, and small inns, such as that at Boat of Garten with one public room, mushroomed into full-blown hotels.

In the Edwardian period, holiday homes for families from the south were built in Kingussie and Aviemore. It was not until 1914 when motor traffic began to have an effect on railway traffic, and subsequent improvements to the Perth-Inverness A9 road, that reduced numbers of holiday-makers came into the area by train. Changes in the type of tourist were seen in the growth of the boarding-house facility, with no fewer than twenty houses of the type being built in Boat of Garten alone by 1939.

The setting up of the Aviemore complex gave the railway a boost; whereas before 1965 Aviemore, for example, was little more than a junction, it now has a considerable significance as a source of traffic in both summer and winter. At the same time, through passenger traffic on the Perth-Inverness line has increased, and the place now buzzes with tourist activity from the estimated one million and more people who visit the area each year.

Now, at the present time, one of the fresh-air lungs of Europe, the Spey valley, is once more at the focus of national attention. Private enterprise and financial speculation placed the area on the map when the York Buildings Company took up the challenge of exploitation to create far-reaching changes of the on-going kind which have lasted two and a half centuries. Today, profit is still the name of the game.

# VII

## WATER OF LIFE

WHATEVER controversy rages around the uses and abuses of Scotch whisky, the fact remains that it is a liquid which has a considerable economic significance in the economy of present-day Scotland. It has been estimated that the value of Scotch whisky in bond represents a sum which exceeds the total gold reserves of Britain. That is no small figure; indeed, it could be said, in comparison, that while the United States of America has its Fort Knox, Britain, or Scotland, has its whisky industry. Whisky is thus a liquid gold, yet it is simply derived from the four elements: air, earth, water and fire, all truly Scottish and, in particular, based largely on a small area of Scotland, in the lower reaches of the Spey valley, where whisky distilleries are so thick on the ground that there are more to the square mile here than in any other part of Scotland. This is perhaps yet another indication of the contribution of the Spey and its tributaries to the socio-economic welfare of small communities in the region.

The origins of whisky are lost somewhere in the dark ages of antiquity. The process of distillation, however, has been recorded as far back as the fourth century B.C., when Aristotle observed that sea water could be made drinkable by distillation. Its advent in Scotland is quite obscure. There is an acceptable suggestion that the ancients of the East, having held for long that cereals and spirits were important ingredients for a long life, revealed their secrets to the passing Celts on their way through Europe to the western fringes. The Celts, being naturally ingenious, combined the two into an elixir to

162

produce 'uisge beatha', the water of life, from which name the word whisky is derived. Evidence points to the Celt settling in Ireland with his new-found discovery, from whence it was transmitted to Scotland. No doubt the old monasteries had a hand in perfecting the techniques, for among the more important centres of distilling today are Islay, Kintyre and Speyside, all sites of the monastic communities of earlier times. In time the liquid came to be recognized as both food and medicine: "that malt spirit which commonly served both for victual and drink". As in Ireland, conditions, particularly in the Highlands of Scotland, were ideal for the production of whisky: fresh mountain air, locally grown barley, nurtured by a warm but kindly sun, pure burn water "off granite through peat", and rich peat which gave off a pungent aroma when burned.

The first mention of whisky in Scotland occurs in an entry in the Exchequer Rolls for the year 1494: "To Friar John Cor, by order of the King, to make aquavitae, VIII bolls of malt". Thereafter, the mention of aqua-vitae occurs with increasing frequency. By 1579, however, there was a problem: the widespread distilling, by folk high-born and low, was creating a famine in grain supplies for solid food. An Act of that year states: "Forasmuch as it appears that victuals shall be scarce this present year, and understanding that there is a great quantity of malt consumed in all parts of this realm in the making of aqua-vitae, this is one great reason for the dearth within the same. It lays down, therefore, that only Earls, Lords, Barons, and Gentlemen, for their own use, shall distil any".

From that time, whisky consistently appears in official records, and, as consistently, is made the subject of repressive measures to restrict its particular appeal to the common folk. The making of whisky was a regular and commonplace activity in many crofting and farmhouse kitchens; at some stage a surplus of liquor was produced, which was either bartered for goods, or simply sold for cash. Thus, its appearance on the market was sufficient to cause the English Government in 1660 to impose a duty of 2d a gallon on the liquor imported to that country. Two decades previously, the Scots Government in Edinburgh produced an Act of Excise (1644) which fixed a sum of 2s 8d Scots per pint for whisky and similar strong liquor; this sum was later reduced to 2s per quart in 1655. A couple of years later saw the beginnings of the operation of the Act of Excise, in the form of the appearance of 'guagers', officers who had the power to gauge or measure containers used in the distillation process. In 1661 the direct tax on home-distilled spirit disappeared and was replaced by an obscure kind of malt tax, itself removed in 1695 when a direct tax was once more imposed. Needless to say, it was this imposition on home spirit which was to create so many political and commercial problems in the ensuing centuries and, indeed, still does.

In the meantime, the golden liquid was being made in sufficient quantities as a secondary occupation in many Highland parishes and was freely available at all times. In the eighteenth century it was quite common to have a refreshment of whisky as part of one's breakfast. Whisky also had some prestige as a special food and medicine. In 1736 it was reported: "The ruddy complexion, nimbleness of these people is not owing to the water drinking but to the aqua vitae, a malt spirit which is commonly used both as victual and drink". Indeed, the fame of whisky spread outside the Highlands to such an extent that in 1832, the year of the great cholera epidemic, it was prescribed as an efficient antidote to the disease.

The Treaty of Union in 1707 between Scotland and England was a watershed in the history of whisky. In that year there was a tax on malt in England but not in Scotland, a point of difference regarded as having such importance that the Articles of Union provided that malt should not be taxed in Scotland; there was also a provision that any malt made in Scotland should not be taxed "during the present war". In 1713 the Treaty of Utrecht brought that war to an end and the Government in Westminster decided to extend the English tax to Scotland, but was thwarted in its efforts in the face of a massive opposition which had 'free malt' as its effective campaign slogan. However, the Government won through in the end and the year 1725 saw Lord Walpole's successful imposition of the tax in Scotland. The ill-considered measure blew up into trouble which became known as the Malt Tax Riots and the trouble mushroomed to such a degree that the military had to be brought in to quell riots all over Scotland. Even General Wade, busy enough on a road-surveying expedition in the Highlands, was diverted in his duties to make haste to Glasgow to impose law and order. Riots in Edinburgh were just as severe; they culminated in the Porteous Riots in which Captain Porteous, a member of the Edinburgh City Guard, was hanged in a lynching in 1736.

Despite these troubles, which at the time had seemed insurmountable, the official mind of government pressed on with a succession of Acts designed to control the making of whisky and to derive a useful revenue from taxes. Inevitably, these moves by officialdom produced a reaction in the making of illicit liquor: the creation of the professional smuggler in the Highlands. Another ill-considered move occurred in 1780 when heavy duties were imposed on wines, which led to a greatly stimulated demand for good whisky, and the manufacture of illicit whisky became an almost universal practice over the next twenty years. Smuggling blossomed to the extent that the licensed distillers found their interests being seriously eroded and fell to producing inferior liquor which failed to restore their former markets. Indeed, the whisky thus produced was so rank that it rarely compared with the 'pure and wholesome' malt liquor which was smuggled down from the Highlands to lowland markets. Further measures were introduced in various Acts of Parliament to control the production of illicit whisky; but these all failed to do anything other than to consolidate the position of the smuggler. Whisky in fact became the most legislated subject in the United Kingdom.

In the year 1814 an Act was passed which required the sum of £10 for a licence for distilling; but the Act prohibited stills of under 500 gallons, which meant that all small home brewers and distillers in the Highland region found themselves on the wrong side of the law, with their main source of income threatened. Colonel Stewart of Garth summed up the situation:

> It is evident that this new law was a complete interdict, as a still of this magnitude would consume more than the disposable grain in the most extensive county within this newly drawn boundary; nor could fuel be obtained for such an establishment without an expense which the commodity could not possibly bear. The sale, too, of the spirits was circumscribed within the same line (Highland distillers were not allowed to market their spirits south of the Grampians), and thus the market which alone could have supported the manufacture was entirely cut off. . . . Thus, hardly any alternative remained but that of having recourse to illicit distillation. These are difficulties of which the Highlanders complain heavily, asserting that nature and the distillery laws present unsurmountable obstacles to the carrying on of a legal traffic. The surplus produce of their (farmers and tenants) agricultural labour will therefore remain on their hands, unless they incur an expense beyond what that article will bear, in conveying so bulky a commodity (grain) to the Lowland market as the raw material, and the drawback of prices on their inferior grain. In this manner, their produce must be disposed of at a great loss, as it cannot legally be manufactured in the country. Hence they resort to smuggling as their only resource. If it indeed be true that this illegal traffic has made such deplorable breaches in the honesty and morals of the people, the revenue drawn from the large distilleries, to which the Highlanders have been made the sacrifice, has been procured at too high a price for the country.

Another comment appears in the Old Statistical Account for Scotland (1796): "Distilling is almost the only method of converting our victual into cash for the payment of rents and servants, and whisky, may, in fact, be called our staple commodity".

The official mind was also made up against another problem: the fact that the products of illicit stills were of a very high quality with a high demand. Some distillers became famous bynames for quality in Scotland – for instance, in the case of George Smith of Glenlivet, whose still was one of some 200 in operation in that area of Speyside which still boasts the largest number of distilleries in Scotland.

George Smith was born in 1792, the son of a Glenlivet farmer. He began his working life as a builder and architect but abandoned these activities when his father died to take over the family farm at Upper Druimin. Settling in there he supervised the small-scale distilling on the farm which, under his direction, became very profitable, mainly due to the excellence of 'Glenlivet', which made its way south through the glens to appreciative samplers of the beverage, among whom was numbered no less a personage than Sir Walter Scott. In the latter's narrative poem, "St Ronan's Well", Sir Bingo treats the Captain and the Doctor to whisky from Glenlivet. After drinking, the Captain says: "By Cot, it is the only liquor for a gentleman to drink in the morning, if he can have the good fortune to come by it, you see". This accolade, it may be remembered, was accorded to a whisky which was at that time regarded by the Government as being illegal. It is said that King George IV, on his visit to Edinburgh in 1822, was introduced to the drink by Sir Walter Scott, and it remained a firm favourite with him for the rest of his life.

Another tribute to Glenlivet was offered by James Hogg, the Ettrick Shepherd: "Give me the real Glenlivet, and I well believe I could mak' drinking toddy oot o' sea-water. The Human mind never tires o' Glenlivet, ony mair than o' caller air. If a body could just find oot the exact proper proportion and quantity that ought to be drunk every day, and keep to that, I verily trow that he might leeve for ever, without dying at a', and that doctors and kirkyards would go oot o'fashion."

To obtain Glenlivet, and the other superb products of the Highland pot still, to such appreciative customers in the south, was no easy business, for the famous George Smith as for others. The presence of the gauger, or exciseman, always added an element of adventure, if not danger, to the smuggler and his regular convoys of hardy Highland ponies with their precious cargoes strapped to their sides, stepping along the whisky trails in the lonely hills. A contemporary account describes these convoys: ". . . in bands of ten to twenty men, with as many horses, with two ankers of whisky on the back of each horse, wending their way, singing in joyous chorus, along the banks of the Avon". On many occasions, interception by excisemen led to fights, often to the death; the profession carried its occupational hazards to the limit. Tales abound of these meetings of both sides of the law. One successful exciseman, Malcolm Gillespie, on the day of his death in 1827, was able to point to forty-two wounds on various parts of his body, all sustained in the course of twenty-eight years' unflinching service.

The year when moonshine became daylight was 1823, when the Illicit Distillation (Scotland) Act came into being, which defined stiff penalties for all offences connected with illicit distilling, for the nth time. Fines of £200 were stipulated in cases where persons were found in possession of unmarked stills, whether they were being used or not. The removal of spirits from one place to another, unless with a permit, also carried a penalty of £200. Excise officers were given greatly increased powers. The Act, in reality, pushed smugglers into a dark and desperate corner. But there was a silver lining to the black clouds, in the form of George Smith, who decided that if he could not operate illegally, then he would make whisky with the blessing of the Act. While he was as tough and as uncompromising as his fellows, he possessed unusual foresight and business acumen for his times and his profession. He therefore took out a licence for his bothy, rebuilt and remodelled his distillery, and set up as a lawful maker of whisky to bring the famous Glenlivet Distillery into official existence. It was no easy transition, however. His fellow smugglers regarded him as a traitor to the time-honoured profession and gave him a rough time of it. His pack-horses were attacked and efforts were made to put him out of business. As he says in his own words:

> About this time (1820) the government, giving its mind to internal reforms, began to awaken to the fact that it might be possible to realize a considerable revenue from the whisky duty

north of the Grampians. No doubt they were helped to this conviction by the grumbling of south-country distillers whose profits were destroyed by the number of kegs which used to come streaming down the mountain passes. The Highlanders had become demoralized through long impunity and the authorities thought it would be safer to use policy rather than force. The question was frequently debated in both Houses of Parliament, and strong representations were made to north-country proprietors to use their influence in the cause of law and order. Pressure of this sort was brought to bear on Alexander, Duke of Gordon, who at length was stirred up to make a reply. The Highlanders, he said, were born distillers; whisky was their beverage from time immemorial, and they would have it and sell it too when tempted by so large a duty.

But, said Duke Alexander, if the legislature would pass an Act affording an opportunity for the manufacture of whisky as good as the smuggled product at a reasonable duty easily payable, he and his brother proprietors of the Highlands would use their best endeavours to put down smuggling and encourage legal distilling. As the outcome of this pledge a Bill was passed in 1823 to include Scotland, sanctioning legal distillation of whisky at a duty of 2s 3d per wine gallon of proof spirit with £10 annual licence for any still above forty gallons; none under that size being allowed.

... A year or two before, the farce of an attempt had been made to inflict a £20 penalty where any quantity of whisky was found manufactured or in process of manufacture. But there was no means of enforcing such a penalty for the smugglers laughed at attempts at seizure; and when the new Act was heard of, both in Glenlivet and in the Highlands of Aberdeenshire, they ridiculed the idea that anyone would be found daring enough to commence distilling in their midst.

The proprietors were very anxious to fulfil their pledge to Government and did everything they could to encourage the commencement of legal distilling; but the desperate character of the smugglers and the violence of their threats deterred anyone for some time. At length, in 1824, I, George Smith, who was then a robust young fellow and not given to be easily 'fleggit', determined to chance it. I was already a tenant of the Duke and received every encouragement from his Grace himself and his factor Mr Skinner. The lookout was an ugly one, though. I was warned by my civil neighbours that they meant to burn the new distillery to the ground, and me in the heart of it. The Laird of Aberlour presented me with a pair of hair trigger pistols worth 10 guineas, and they were never out of my belt for years. I got together two or three stout fellows for servants, armed them with pistols, and let it be known everywhere that I would fight for my place to the last shot. I had a pretty good character as a man of my word and, through watching by turns every night for years, we contrived to save the distillery from the fate so freely predicted for it.

But I often, both at kirk and market, had rough times of it among the glen people; and if it had not been for the Laird of Aberlour's pistols, I don't think I should be telling you this story now. In 1825 and 1826 three more legal distilleries were commenced in the glen, but the smugglers very soon succeeded in frightening away their occupants, none of whom ventured to hold on a single year in the face of threats uttered so freely against them. Threats were not the only weapons used. In 1825 a distillery which had just been started near the Banks o' Dee at the head of Aberdeenshire was burnt to the ground with all its outbuildings and appliances, and the distiller had a very narrow escape from being roasted in his own kiln. The country was in a desperately lawless state at this time. The riding officers of the revenue were the mere sport of the smugglers, and nothing was more common than for them to be shown a still at work and then coolly defied to make a seizure.

Smith's distillery survived these hard times and exists today as one of the best known stills in Scotland with the equally famous 'Glenlivet' able to delight as many palates today as it did when the brew was an illicit elixir. However, Smith's problems were brought to the surface in later years when he had to meet opponents of a different kind: when other distilleries began to be built in Glenlivet and they tried to cash in on the reputation of the original 'Glenlivet'. In 1880, after a long legal tussle, a High Court order was secured making Smith's whisky the only one entitled to the name 'Glenlivet' without a hyphenated prefix, which includes the true name of a particular distillery.

Long before George Smith's efforts to make whisky-distilling an honourable profession, Nature had been at work to provide the Spey valley with all the necessary ingredients which the 'cunning chemists' transformed into whisky. The most southerly distillery is at Dalwhinnie, owned by Distillers Company Limited, the largest combine in the whisky business. Farther north there are the Speyside distilleries at Kingussie and Balmenach, at Cromdale. This latter distillery has an interesting history, and is on the site of an original smuggler's bothy. When Alfred Barbard toured all the distilleries in the United Kingdom and Ireland, he was impressed by the site, created by choice and not by accident: "The range of the Cromdale hills, some seven or eight miles long, stretched out before us. In days gone by these activities were the favourite haunt of smugglers, who chose the locality on account of the numerous hill-streams, whose waters are of fine quality and highly suitable for distilling purposes." He was shown round the operations (in 1885). He was

. . . first directed to the double-arched cavern, dug deep in the hill, fifty yards from the Distillery, in which at one time a noted band of smugglers carried out their operations. . . . It possessed an underground spring, wherein the little coil or worm, which condensed the precious spirit, was laid, and at a lower level it dripped into a receiver, made out of an earthen jar some two feet high, with a wooden lid thereon. The little copper still stood on a furnace made with the loose stones that had fallen from the rock behind, and the Mash-tun had originally been a wash-tub. The place was totally dark, and no light was ever permitted except that which came from the furnace fire. One night the Revenue Officers made a raid on the place, and knowing the desperate men they had to deal with, were all well armed. On their arrival, they crept stealthily through the narrow entrance to the cave, following the informer, who knew the place well. Meanwhile, the smugglers unconscious of the close proximity of their enemies, were scattered about the cavern, some sleeping, others smoking, and one or two looking after the distilling operations.
One of their number opened the furnace door to replenish the

fire, and the momentary flash of light revealed to his comrade the figures of the officers stealing up on them. With great presence of mind he instantly unhooked the pipe which connected the furnace with a concealed chimney in the roof, and then fired off his pistol at the nearest enemy. The noise alarmed the gang who escaped from the cave, under cover of the dense smoke emitted from the open furnace. The officers were dumbfounded, and almost choked, but the informer quickly replaced the chimney-pipe, and as soon as the smoke had dispersed, the officers lighted their lamps from the furnace fire, and proceeded to demolish the place . . . This scare broke up and scattered the gang, and since that time there has been very little smuggling in this district.

This distillery was established on a legal basis in 1824 and produces Balmenach-Glenlivet Highland malt whisky. It is on the periphery of a tight ring of producers of bright golden water, the proprietary brand names of which roll off the tongue as smoothly as a well-composed poem stuffed full with imagery and able to stir the imagination with flights of tastebud fancies:

Tormore, Glenfarclas-Glenlivet, Craggamore, Imperial, Knockando, Tamdhu-Glenlivet, Cardow, Glenrothes-Glenlivet, Caperdonich, Glen Grant-Glenlivet, Speyburn, Glen Elgin, Ben Riach-Glenlivet, Glenburgie-Glenlivet, Mannochmore, Glenlossie, Miltonduff-Glenlivet, Glen Moray-Glenlivet, Linkwood, Longmorn-Glenlivet, Coleburn, Glen Spey, Macallan-Glenlivet, Craigellachie, Convalmore, Balvenie, Dufftown-Glenlivet, Glenfiddich, Glendullan, Mortlach, Aberlour-Glenlivet, Glenallachie, Benrinnes, Dailuaine, The Glenlivet, Tamnavullin-Glenlivet, Tomintoul-Glenlivet.

What is whisky? Chemists know what it contains, yet are unable, in a laboratory situation, to produce a liquid which can compare with a product based on centuries of knowledge and cunning. Imitation being a form of flattery, there have been many attempts to produce whisky overseas, for instance in Japan; but all have failed to yield a drink which can match up to the real stuff. Water is not, on its own, the secret, for there are a number of distilleries which make use of the same source of water, yet their products have distinctive tastes. Barley from the same source can be treated to yield a different end product. The peat used to dry malted barley differs from place to place in the aroma it gives off when burned: that might be part of the secret. But then the air of the Highland hills and glens seeks to establish a place for itself in the formula. Last, but certainly not least, the distiller represents a continuous element in the distilling process. Is the secret in the sherry casks used to mature whisky? Again, it is anyone's guess. Little wonder then that whisky has been the subject of prose, poetry and song over the centuries and will always remain a close friend to those who ignore the attempts of politicians and speculative interests to impose iniquitous duties on their favourite drink.

There are three principal varieties of whisky recognized in Scotland today: malt, grain and blended. For the descriptions of these I am indebted to an old friend, Iain Cameron Taylor of Inverness, who has spent a lifetime of association with the liquid, and made it into a special study to the extent that he has built himself a detailed scaled-down model of a malt distillery which he fondly hopes one day, by some magic, will grow into the real thing. Such is the inspiring effect of malt.

Malt whisky, usually Highland but it may be Lowland, is made entirely from a watery extract of malted barley, fermented by the addition of yeast and then twice distilled in the characteristic onion-shaped pot-stills, from which the flavoured alcohol is driven off by heat. The still has to be recharged after each distillation. The chief difference between the two classes of malt is that the Highland one has its malted barley dried in the kiln over a peat fire. It is the combustion fume of the peat which endows the whisky with that subtle 'smokiness' and which, in discreet combination with other flavours, is the hall mark of a genuine Highland whisky. Malt whisky takes from ten to fifteen years in oak casks to mature properly. . . . Although today the larger proportion of malt whisky goes for blending, a growing number of distilleries now have their 'single' or unblended malts specially bottled to meet the demand – and the taste of those who are sufficiently discriminating to select, with full knowledge of its locality and background, the particular whisky of their choice and delight.

Grain whisky is mostly made from imported maize (American corn), but rye and oats can also be used. After mashing, with the addition of a little malted barley, it is fermented and then distilled in a Coffey or patent-still, where the alcohol is driven off by steam. It is possible with this type of still to produce a spirit with a 95 percent alcohol content in one continuous operation. This is the means by which the bulk of our industrial alcohol is manufactured and at one time a large proportion of the raw product went to London to be made into gin or methylated spirits. It can be argued that its value in whisky distilling is more doubtful and for a long time the question of whether or not spirit made in a patent-still was entitled to the name of 'whisky' was one which exercised the minds of those who were genuinely interested in the honour of the traditional liquor. It took a Royal Commission in 1909 to recognize the newcomer and to give it (recklessly perhaps and much to the chagrin of the Highland distillers) equal status with that unique and exquisite result of centuries of dedicated knowledge and practice. Grain whisky is lighter and chemically purer than malt whisky, but has a less distinctive flavour. It matures more quickly but does not improve in the cask to anything like the extent of malt whisky and, although cheaper to make, it is wrong to describe it as a neutral spirit. It is now generally drunk as whisky but it is used for blending with malt whiskies.

Blended whisky is a mixture of matured and grain whiskies, to secure the lighter purity of the grain with the unmistakable flavour of the malts. The practice of blending pot-still and patent-still whiskies began about 1860 largely for the home, or southern market. . . . Blending in itself is a skilled industry, for as many as thirty or more different malts may be mixed with the almost neutral, or 'silent' grain spirit.

As mentioned already, the major Highland malt whisky producing area is fed by the waters of the River Spey and its tributaries. It lies in the Counties of Nairn, Moray and Banff, and extends about fifty miles east to west and about twenty-five miles south of the Moray Firth. Both the ranges of the Monadhliath and Grampian Mountains contribute their waters to the northern reaches of Strathspey. Not content with this distinction, Speyside whiskies are distinctive in themselves from other Highland malts (those produced, for example, on Islay are heavy and peaty in flavour) being lighter in 'weight', yet carry their character on the palate in a succession of tastes: peat, scent, and malt, all slipping down the throat in a smooth, full-flavoured trickle – water of life indeed. Little wonder that Robert Burns summed up this unique liquid:

> Freedom and whisky gang thegither,
> Tak aff your dram'

The Gael, however, was not without literary respect for his whisky:

> Is coisiche na h-oidhche thu
> Gu leapannan na maighdeannan;
> Righ! gur h-iomadh loinn a th'ort
> Gu coibhneas thoirt a gruagach.
> (You are the prowler of the night
> To the beds of virgins;
> Oh God! what powers you have
> To gain kindness from girls.)

NOTE: The following distillery town and villages, some are in fact simply human settlements clustered round the distillery, of Speyside are: Aberlour, Keith, Cromdale, Dufftown, Rothes, Knockando, Dufftown, Ballindalloch, Craigellachie, Carron, Glenlivet, Tomnavoulin, and Advie. Some distilleries offer conducted tours round their operations with the possibility of a sample at the end of the visit. Some distilleries have also set up visitor centres, such as that at Glenfarclas-Glenlivet at Ballindalloch, which show the various stages in the process of making malt whisky.

Like all industries with an international market, whisky distilling is being continually subjected to financial pressures, as seen in take-over bids. An example of this was seen in connection with the Glen Grant Distillery at Rothes. New stills were opened in 1978 at a cost of around £500,000 to increase production by about one million gallons each year. In 1970 several of the Spey distilleries amalgamated to form The Glenlivet Distillers Ltd, but to ensure their future survival the company had to sell out to Seagrams, the Canadian group for £50 million, ending the Grant family connection which stretched back 144 years. However, those who favour Glen Grant are assured by the new owners that the malt produced will not change. The same care in production, in the buying of top quality barley, peat from traditional areas, and even water from the same burn, will continue as before, to ensure that the taste of Glen Grant will continue to delight its devotees.

# APPENDIX

## THE 'SPEY' NAME

THE derivation of the name 'Spey' is obscure. The most acceptable meaning is from the Gaelic word '*speidh*', meaning rapidity or strength, certainly two characteristics of the river. One authority has suggested that the name is derived from the Teutonic 'spe' (sputum) "because of the rapidity of it raiseth much foam and froth". In an ancient map of Ptolemy, A.D. 150, the river is shown flowing into "Tuesses Aestuarium". A later map of the fourteenth century, made by Richard of Cirencester (1336), shows the Spey with the name of "Tuessis"; a Roman station about thirty miles from the river mouth bears the same name as the river, which is depicted as flowing into "Tuessis Aestuarium". There is a tradition that the Spey had its outflow into the Moray Firth some three miles west of Kingston, evidence for this being taken on the basis of a small cairn known locally as Spey's Law. But there seems to be no physical evidence to suggest that this was ever the case. That the mouth of the river was a mile west of its present position is suggested in a Paper in the *Journal of the Royal Scottish Geographical Society*: "So far no good evidence has been found to support the old tradition that the Spey once ran westward in a narrow cut parallel to the shore, and entered the sea three miles distant from its present mouth and opposite to a hill [*sic*] called Spey's Law. Many centuries ago it may have entered the sea about a mile west of the present mouth where air photographs show that the shingle forms a number of hooks curving into a strip of low lying ground, marked as a morass in McGill's map of 1725."

Locally this morass is known as the Streeds, and there is strong evidence that they may mark an ancient bed of the Spey.

# BIBLIOGRAPHY

Alexander, H., *The Cairngorms* (Scottish Mountaineering Club, Edinburgh, various editions)

Allan, J. R., *North-east Lowlands of Scotland* (London, 1952 and 1974)

Anderson, G., *Kingston-on-Spey* (Edinburgh, 1957)

Baddeley, M. J. B., *The Highlands of Scotland* (London, 1882)

Barnard, A., *The Whisky Distilleries of the United Kingdom*, London, 1887; new edition David and Charles, 1969)

Barron, R., "Baideanach", *Trans. Gaelic Society of Inverness*, Vols. XXXIX, XL and XLII

Blackie, J., *Altavona* (London, 1883)

Blaikie, W. B., *Itinerary of Prince Charles Edward Stuart* (Edinburgh, 1897) Scottish History Society

——, *Origins of the Forty-five;* (Edinburgh, 1916 and 1975) Scottish History Society

Bremner, A., "Origin of the Scottish River System"; *Scottish Geographical Society Magazine*, Vol. LVIII

Bulloch, J., *The Life of the Celtic Church* (Edinburgh, 1963)

Bulloch, J. M. *Sporting Visitors to Badenoch* (Inverness, 1931)

Calderwood, W. L., *The Salmon Rivers and Lochs of Scotland* (London, 1921)

*Celtic Magazine, The,* "Spey", Vol. V; "The Battle of Invernahavon", Vol. V; "Laggan", Vol. V.

Corson, F. R., *Beyond the Great Glen* (Edinburgh, 1950)

Cramond, W., *The Church of Speymouth* (Elgin, 1890)

Daiches, D., *Scotch Whisky* (London, 1969)

Dunnett, H., *Invera'an: A Strathspey Parish* (Paisley, 1919)

Fenton, A., "The Currach in Scotland", *Scottish Studies*, Vol. 16, Part I

Finlay, R., *The Unknown Highlands* (London, 1970)
Firsoff, V. A., *The Cairngorms on Foot and Ski* (London, 1949)
Forsyth, W., *In the Shadow of Cairngorm* (Inverness, 1900)
Fraprie, F. R., *Castles and Keeps of Scotland* (London, 1907)
Fraser Darling, F., *Natural History in the Highlands and Islands* (London, 1947)
Gaffney, V., *The Lordship of Strathavon*, 3rd Spalding Club Edition (Aberdeen, 1960)
*Glenlivet: Annals of the Distillery* (Aberdeen, 1924 and 1959)
Gordon, S., *Highlands of Scotland* (London, 1951)
——, *The Cairngorm Hills of Scotland* (London, 1926)
Grant, I. F., *Highland Folk Ways* (London, 1961)
——, *The Clan Grant* (Edinburgh, 1955)
Grant, E., *Memoirs of a Highland Lady* (London, 1898 and 1950)
Grant, J. S., *Highland Villages* (London, 1977)
Grant, E., *Letters from the Mountains* (London, 1807)
Gray, A., *The Big Grey Man of Ben Macdhui* (Aberdeen, 1970)
Grimble, A., *The Salmon Rivers of Scotland* (London, 1913)
Haldane, A. R. B., *The Drove Roads of Scotland* (Edinburgh, 1952; David and Charles new edition, 1973)
——, *New Ways through the Glens* Edinburgh, 1962, David and Charles new edition, 1973)
Hillman, R. N., *The Making of a Scottish Landscape* (London, 1975)
Hinxman, L. W., "The River Spey"; *Scottish Geographical Society Magazine*, Vol. XVII
Inverness Board of Advertising, *The Book of the Highlands* (Glasgow, 1937)
Inverness Field Club, "River Spey", Vol. VI
Institute of Geological Sciences, *The Grampian Highlands* (Edinburgh, 1966)
Kerr, J., "Old Grampian Highways"; *Trans. of Gaelic Society of Inverness*, Vol. XLIX
Laird, R. A., *Some Low Level Walks in Strathspey* (Aviemore, 1976)
Lauder, T. D., *The Great Floods of August 1829* (Elgin, 1873)

Lindsay, J. M., "Some Aspects of the Timber Supply in the Highlands, 1700-1850", *Scottish Studies*, Vol. 19

Lindsay, M., *The Discovery of Scotland* (London, 1964)

London, Midland & Scottish Railway, *Handbook to the Highland Section* (Inverness, 1924)

Longmuir, J., *Speyside* (London, 1860)

MacBain, A., "Placenames of Badenoch", *Trans. Gaelic Society of Inverness*, Vol. XVI

McConnochie, A. I., *Guide to Aviemore and Vicinity* (Aviemore, 1902)

——, *Strathspey* (Aberdeen, 1902)

MacDonald, M. A., "Drovering", *Trans. Gaelic Society of Inverness*, Vol. XLIX

MacDonald, M., *The Covenanters in Moray and Ross* (Inverness, 1892)

MacGregor, A. A., *The Buried Barony* (London, 1949)

——, *The Peat-fire Flame* (Edinburgh, 1937)

MacGregor, J., "Abhainn Spé", *Trans. Gaelic Society of Inverness*, Vol. XVII

Mackintosh, A., "The History of Strathspeys and Reels", *Trans. Gaelic Society of Inverness*, Vol. XXVII

Mackintosh, H. B., *Pilgrimages in Moray* (Elgin, 1924)

MacMillan, H., *Rothiemurchus* (London, 1907)

MacLean, C. I., *The Highlands* (Inverness, 1975)

McNeill, P. and Nicholson, R., eds *An Historical Atlas of Scotland, c. 400 – c. 1600* (St Andrews, 1975)

Macpherson, H., *A Scots Scrapbook* (Inverness, 1973)

Macpherson, A. T., "An Old Highland Parish Register (Laggan)," *Scottish Studies;* Vols. 11 and 12

Macpherson, A., "The Old Church of Kingussie", *Celtic Magazine* Vol. XIII (Inverness, 1888)

Macpherson, A., "Badenoch in Olden Times", *Trans. Gaelic Society of Inverness*, Vol. XIII

——, "Badenoch, From Old Ecclesiastical Records", *Trans. Gaelic Society of Inverness*, Vol. XII

——, "Sketches of Badenoch", *Trans. Gaelic Society of Inverness*, 1Vols XIV and XV

MacRow, B., *Speyside to Deeside* (Edinburgh, 1956)
McVean, D. N., and Lockie, J. D., *Ecology and Land Use in Upland Scotland* (Edinburgh, 1969)
Mitchell, A., *Pre-1855 Gravestone Inscriptions on Speyside* (for the Scottish Genealogy Society, 1977)
Mitchell, J., *Reminiscences of my Life in the Highlands* (1883 and David and Charles, 1971)
Moir, D. G., *Scottish Hill Tracks: Northern Scotland* (Edinburgh, 1975)
Murdoch, J., *Speyside, its Scenery and Antiquities* (Elgin, 1876)
Murray, D., *The York Buildings Company* (1883 and Edinburgh, 1973)
Murray, D. C., "Notes on the Parish of Duthil", *Trans. Gaelic Society of Inverness*, Vol. XLIII
Nairne, D., *Memorable Highland Floods of the Nineteenth Century* (Inverness, 1895)
Napier Commission into Crofting Conditions, *Report* (Edinburgh, 1884)
Nethersole-Thompson, D, and Watson, A., *The Cairngorms* (London, 1974)
Newbiggin, N. I., *The Kingussie District: A Geographical Study* (London, 1906)
O'Dell, A. C., and Walton, K., *The Highlands and Islands of Scotland* (Edinburgh, 1962)
Omand, D., ed, *The Moray Book* (Edinburgh, 1976)
Quigley, H., *The Highlands of Scotland* (London, 1936)
Rennie, J., *Romantic Strathspey* (London, 1956)
Robertson, B., *Some Straths and Glens of Inverness-shire* (1975)
Ross, J., *Whisky* (London, 1970)
Royal Society for the Protection of Birds, *Ospreys and Speyside Wildlife*, (Edinburgh, 1973)
Scottish Youth Hostels Association, *Guide to the Cairngorms* (Stirling, 1972)
Scottish Development Department, *Report: The Cairngorm Area* (Edinburgh, 1971)
Seton, M., *Moray Past and Present* [Collection of photographs] (Elgin, 1978)

Shepherd, N., *The Living Mountain* (Aberdeen, 1977)

Sillett, S. W., *Illicit Scotch* (Aberdeen, 1970)

Simper, R., *Scottish Sail* (David and Charles, 1974)

Sinclair, N. T., *Strathspey Railway Guide Book* (Boat of Garten, 1975)

Somers, R., *Letters from the Highlands on the Famine of 1846* (1848 and Inverness, 1977)

Smith, C. M., *Strathspey: Highways and Byways* (Elgin, 1957)

Statistical Accounts of Scotland, (Counties of Moray and Nairn) (1796, 1840 and Glasgow, 1956)

Steven H. M. and Carlisle, R., *Native Pinewoods and Scotland* (Edinburgh, 1959)

Stewart, W. G., *Lectures on the Mountains* (London, 1860)

Swire, O., *The Highlands and their Legends* (Edinburgh, 1963)

Tegner, H., *A Naturalist on Speyside* (London, 1971)

Taylor, I. C., *Highland Whisky* (Inverness, 1968)

——, *Highland Communications* (Inverness, 1969)

Thompson, F., *The Highlands and Islands* (London, 1974)

Ward, Lock & Co., *Inverness and Speyside* (London, 1920)

Webster, M. M., *Flora of Moray, Nairn and East Inverness* (Aberdeen, 1978)

Wilson, R., *Scotch, Its History and Romance* (David and Charles, 1973)

Wood, W., *The Secret of Spey* (Edinburgh, 1930)

Woodburn, D. A., ed., *Glen More Forest Park* (Edinburgh, 1975)

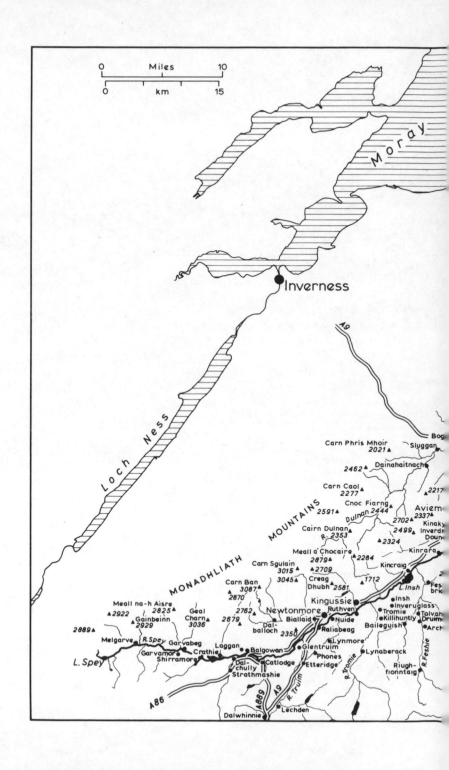

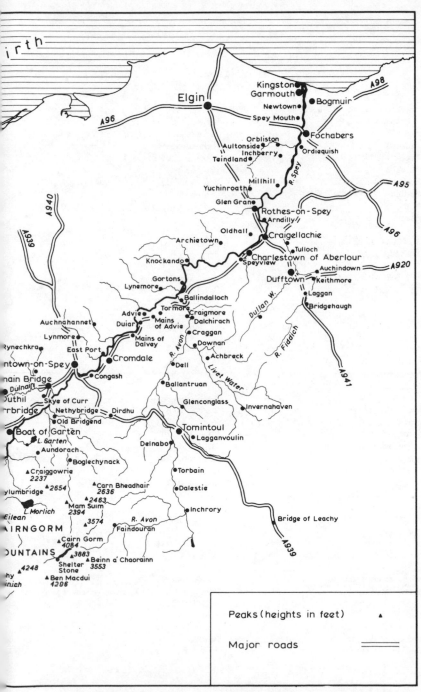

irth

Kingston
Garmouth
Elgin
Bogmuir
A98
Newtown
A96
Spey Mouth
Fochabers
Orbliston
Aultonside
Inchberry
Ordiequish
Teindland
A95
Millhill
Yuchinroath
R. Spey
Glen Grant
A96
Rothes-on-Spey
Arndilly
A940
Oldhall
Craigellachie
A939
Archietown
Tulloch
Knockando
Charlestown of Aberlour
A920
Speyview
Gortons
Auchindown
Lynemore
Dufftown
Keithmore
Ballindalloch
Laggan
Tormore
Dullan W.
Bridgehaugh
Advie
Craigmore
Mains
Duiar
of Advie
Dalchirach
Auchnahannet
Craggan
R. Fiddich
Lynmore
Mains of
Downan
Rynechkra
Dalvey
East Port
Achbreck
A941
Cromdale
Dell
Livet Water
ntown-on-Spey
Ballantruan
nain Bridge
Congash
Dulnain
uthil
Skye of Curr
Glenconglass
Invernahaven
rbridge
Nethybridge
Dirdhu
Old Bridgend
Boat of Garten
Tomintoul
L. Garten
Lagganvoulin
Aundorach
Delnabo
Boglechynack
Craiggowrie
Torbain
2237
ylumbridge
2654
Carn Bheadhair
Dalestie
2636
2463
L.Morlich
Mam Suim
Inchrory
ilean
2394
3574
R. Avon
Bridge of Leachy
IRNGORM
Faindouran
Cairn Gorm
4084
UNTAINS
3883
A939
Beinn a' Chaorainn
Shelter
3553
hy
4248
Stone
nich
Ben Macdui
1206

Peaks (heights in feet)     ▲

Major roads

*Based with permission on the Ordnance Survey, Crown Copyright Reserved.*

# INDEX